THE PSYCHOLOGY OF BLACKS

An African-American Perspective

Second Edition

JOSEPH L. WHITE, Ph.D.

THOMAS A. PARHAM, Ph.D.

HALFORD H. FAIRCHILD, Ph.D.
2271 West Twenty-fifth Street
Los Angeles, CA 90018

PRENTICE HALL
Englewood Cliffs, New Jersey 07632

Library of Congress Cataloging-in-Publication Data

White, Joseph L., [date]
   The psychology of Blacks : an African-American perspective / Joseph
L. White, Thomas A. Parham.—2nd ed.
   p. cm.
    Bibliography: p.
    Includes index.
    ISBN 0-13-733791-4
   1. Afro-Americans—Psychology. I. Parham, Thomas A. (Thomas
Anthony), [date]. II. Title.
E185.625.W47 1990
305.8'96073—dc20   89–16070
                                             CIP

Editorial/production supervision and
interior design: Fred Dahl
Cover design: Wanda Lubelska
Manufacturing buyer: Robert Anderson

© 1990, 1984 by Prentice-Hall, Inc.
A Division of Simon & Schuster
Englewood Cliffs, New Jersey 07632

Printed in the United States of America
10 9 8 7 6 5 4 3 2

ISBN 0-13-733791-4

Prentice-Hall International (UK) Limited, *London*
Prentice-Hall of Australia Pty. Limited, *Sydney*
Prentice-Hall Canada Inc., *Toronto*
Prentice-Hall Hispanoamericana, S.A., *Mexico*
Prentice-Hall of India Private Limited, *New Delhi*
Prentice-Hall of Japan, Inc., *Tokyo*
Simon & Schuster Asia Pte. Ltd., *Singapore*
Editora Prentice-Hall do Brasil Ltda., *Rio de Janeiro*

CONTENTS

FOREWORD

In writing the foreword for the first edition of *The Psychology of Blacks*, Professor Reginald L. Jones commented on the important role played by Professor Joseph White in marking the transition of scholarship on the psychology of Blacks from a deficiency-based Euro-centric perspective to alternative models developed by Black social scientists, which have more explanatory power to account for the behavior of Black people. Professor Jones stated, "It is entirely fitting, then, that Professor White, whose seminal papers captured the need for a psychology of Afro-Americans, and who has chronicled important developments in this field, now takes upon himself the task of presenting an integrated and conceptually coherent psychological portrait of Afro-Americans."

The success of the first edition, as well as the appealing hypotheses and propositions that it posed, formed the catalyst for the writing of this second edition. Professor White is joined in this work by Dr. Thomas Parham, a protege who has become an outstanding psychologist in his own right. Together, this cross-generational team has built significantly on the foundation of the first edition.

The "Basic Assumptions and Historical Backdrop" of the first edition is incorporated into a more extensive conceptual chapter on "The Emergence of Contemporary Black Psychology." The revision of the chapter on the Black family and its positioning earlier in the book is another important enhancement, since it provides further context for the issues addressed in the remaining chapters. The chapter in the first edition on "Stages in the Psychological Development of Black Youth" gives way to a more contemporary piece on "The Struggle for Identity Congruence in African-Americans," a major area of research for Dr. Parham. Also new to this edition are chapters on educational achievement and mental health service delivery, both of which are solid contributions.

One of the most significant new features of the second edition is the chapter on "Contemporary Issues Confronting the Black Community," which presents a scholarly, yet very human, perspective on everyday concerns: the endangered Black male, male-female relationships, the development of social competencies, and responding to the challenges of maintaining an Afro-centric perspective and value system in a Euro-centric environment.

White and Parham have accomplished the difficult task of adding further to the contributions of the first edition to the scholarship on African-American psychology. The second edition retains the authentic representation of Black life and the readability of the first edition, while responding effectively to critics who expressed the need for more research references to support certain assertions and conceptualizations.

The second edition of *The Psychology of Blacks* represents essential reading for students, lay persons, professionals, and researchers who want to acquire a comprehensive introduction to Black psychology.

HORACE MITCHELL

PREFACE

The first edition of *The Psychology of Blacks* was a solid contribution to the literature, providing readers with a unique look at the conceptual paradigms, cultural themes, and psychological constructs used to understand the thoughts, feelings, and behaviors of African-Americans. It has received much praise, both for the content presented by Dr. White, as well as for the process used to convey the ideas. Indeed, countless individuals have commented on the very "down-to-earth," "readable," "captivating," "enlightening," and "novel-like" way the first edition attempted to capture the African-American experience in America.

The irony of the first edition was that one of the book's primary strengths also served as its major source of criticism. The clear, understandable, and almost conversational style of writing in the book opened the door to questions regarding its utility as an example of rigorous scholarship. The text was easy for students to read and understand; consequently, instructors experienced little difficulty in encouraging students to read the book. Conversely, reviewers and other scholars have asked why many of the points made in the book were not empirically supported with data. In some respects, the critical feedback was absolutely accurate; many of the ideas and concepts presented in the first edition could have been supplemented and supported by empirical evidence. We are also mindful, however, that to assume anecdotic experiences are not valid and opinions are mere rhetoric if not supported by absolute empirical evidence is a very western, Euro-centric perspective. Indeed, we would argue that observation, based on life experiences, does have a place in African-American scholarship.

We are strong believers in the fact that life, at its best, is a creative synthesis of opposites. Therefore, we have taken both the compliments and the criticisms of the first edition and attempted to blend the perspectives of rigor and relevance into one project.

The result is the second edition. Chapter One discusses the emergence of contemporary Black psychology and attempts to explore the issue of why a psychological perspective, specific to African-American people, is necessary. Chapter Two discusses issues relevant to the Black family in America. Particular attention is given to both a critique of the existing pathology-oriented Black family literature, as well as a discussion of how social forces and environmental realities combine to impact the Black family. Chapter Three attempts to articulated our beliefs about identity development in African-Americans. It draws on the work of several African-American psychologists who are in the forefront of identity development research relative to Black people. Chapter Four, a discussion of the major themes and language/communication styles of African-Americans, has been reprinted from the first edition, with editing. Chapter Five presents a discussion of the psychosocial and cultural factors that we believe impact on the academic achievement of African-American youngsters. In addition to a discussion of the educational attainment trends among Blacks, consideration is also given to concrete steps that can be taken to help support the educational endeavors of our youth. We also thank Dr. William

Parham for his assistance with this chapter, as several of the ideas are derived from a previous work that he co-authored. Chapter Six focuses on mental health issues as they relate to African-Americans. In perhaps our boldest assertions of the text, we share our perspective on how cultural congruence is the key to mental health. We also share our ideas for appropriate clinical service delivery strategies with an African-American population. Chapter Seven contains a discussion of several contemporary issues we believe will continue to impact various segments of the Black community into the 1990s. While no attempt is made to resolve the issues presented in this last chapter, we do believe that the ideas can serve as a catalyst for future dialogue among members of the Black community.

This second edition continues to follow the notion that a distinctive African cultural influence has persisted, despite the years of oppression, discrimination, and injustice that characterized the African-American experience in this country. We believe that this cultural heritage has much to contribute to the understanding, maintenance, and survival of the African-American psyche; therefore, one will recognize our attempts to encourage Black people to embrace these cultural prerequisites in every dimension of our lives.

It is also worth noting that this second edition of *The Psychology of Blacks* is a product of collaboration of two generations of Black psychologists. Our personal and professional relationships are mirror images of the values of interdependence, mentorship, mutual support, creative synthesis of differences, vitality, resourcefulness, and hope for the future despite the constant struggle ahead, which is discussed on the following pages. This blending of generational perspectives and differences is captured in the writing styles, the interchangeable use of terms "Black" and "African-American," and the focus on self-identification and self-determination evidenced throughout the book. It is our hope that students, professionals, and members of the nonprofessional public will find the text beneficial in furthering their understanding of the psychological issues that impact on the lives of African-American people.

THOMAS A. PARHAM
JOSEPH L. WHITE

ACKNOWLEDGMENTS AND DEDICATION

To Dorothy Lee and Sadie, our mothers, for teaching us to successfully negotiate the pathways to productivity and creativity, and helping us integrate the African and the American world views into our own psychological space. For Joseph L. Sr. and William D., our fathers, who served as instruments of the Creator in transmitting to us, in collaboration with our mothers, the breath of life. To Davida and Lois, our wives, for the patience, understanding, encouragement, and support they provided during the many months it took to complete this project.

Next, we would like to thank our secretaries, Debbie LePage and Edna Mejia, for their assistance in preparing the early and final drafts of the manuscript.

We also would like to thank Dr. Horace Mitchell, the Vice-Chancellor for Student Affairs at University of California, Irvine for his constructive feedback at critical stages in the preparation of this book. We also owe Dr. Mitchell a debt of gratitude for his contribution in writing the Foreword to this second edition.

This book is dedicated to Aldrich Manceo Patterson, Sr., who recently passed on from this world to join the community of our ancestors. He was a father figure to many of us whose fathers were not physically of psychologically available because of the systematic destruction of Black males in American society. To us, he was more than just a "good brother"; he was an inspirational force who modeled the principles of responsibility, resourcefulness, strength, humor, and love, which are discussed on the pages of this text.

Most importantly, we give thanks to the Creator and hope that our words and deeds reflect His way.

JOSEPH L. WHITE
THOMAS A. PARHAM

CHAPTER ONE

THE EMERGENCE OF CONTEMPORARY BLACK PSYCHOLOGY

The first edition of *The Psychology of Blacks* (White, 1984) used as its guiding theme the premise that a unique, coherent, persistent psychological perspective or world view exists that is uniquely African-American. According to White, the African-American perspective can be seen in the behaviors, attitudes, feelings, expressive patterns, and values of Black people. Furthermore, it provides Blacks with a way of interpreting reality and relating to others, as well as a general design for living. The second edition continues to hold to the same assumption.

DEFINITIONS

Those who have not had the benefit of reading the first edition, or who are otherwise unfamiliar with the concept of a Black psychological perspective, may be asking themselves, "What is this discipline called Black Psychology?" Perhaps the most logical place to begin is with a definition of the construct (psychology of blacks) and with a discussion of why a Black psychological perspective is necessary.

Psychology has been around for thousands of years, and dates back to ancient KMT (African-Egyptian) civilizations

(Nobles, 1986). Nobles (1986) reminds us that, in its truest form, psychology was defined by Ancient Africans as the study of the soul or spirit. He writes:

> A summary reading of our ancient mythology reveals that ancient Egyptian thought can be characterized as possessing (1) "ideas of thought" which represent the human capacity to have "will" and to invent or create; (2) "ideas of command" which represent the human capacity to have "intent" and to produce that which one wills. Parenthetically these two, will and intent, are the characteristics of divine spirit and would serve as the best operationalization of human intelligence. [Nobles, 1986, p. 46]

Nobles further asserts that the psychology borrowed from Africa, and popularized in Europe and America (the so-called Western psychology), in some respects, represents a distortion of Ancient African-Egyptian thought. What the Ancients believed was the study of the soul or spirit was translated by Europeans into the study of only one element of a person's psychic nature, the mind. Thus, the term "psychology" (in a Western context)—dependent for its meaning on the Greek word *psyche* (meaning mind) and the fragment *ology* (meaning knowledge)—is generally assumed to be a study of human behavior.

As a discipline, therefore, psychology—like history, anthropology, and many other fields of study—has fallen victim to the attempts by many to both (a) destroy and/or otherwise erase its historical connections to ancient Africa, and (b) transplant its roots into European civilization. Traditional psychology, as we know it in this country, was assumed to extend back only as far as the laboratories of Wilhelm Wundt in Germany around 1879. In its simplest form, traditional psychology was an attempt to explain the behaviors of Europeans from a European frame of reference. After becoming popularized in America, Euro-American scientists began to engage in the same practice of defining and understanding the behaviors of various Euro-American peoples.

In their attempt to understand the mind and behaviors of their people, many European and Euro-American scholars began to develop theories of human behavior (i.e., Freud, Jung, Rogers). Theories are sets of abstract concepts that people assign to a group of facts or events in order to explain them. Theories of personality and/or psychology, then, are organized systems of belief that help us to understand human nature and make sense out of scientific data and other behavioral phenomena. It is important to realize, however, that theories are based on the philosophies, customs, mores, and norms of a given culture. This has certainly been true for the theories that emerged out of the Euro-American frame of reference.

In their attempt to explain what they considered to be "universal human phenomena," Euro-American psychologists implicitly and explicitly began to establish a normative standard of behavior against which all other cultural groups would be measured. What emerged as normal or abnormal, sane or insane, relevant or irrelevant, was always in comparison to how closely a particular thought or behavior paralleled that of white Europeans and/or European-Americans. For many White social scientists and psychologists, the word "different," when applied to people, became synonymous with "deficient," rather than simply different.

The foundation for an authentic Black psychology is an accurate understanding of the Black family, its African roots, historical development and contemporary expressions, and its impact on the psychological development and socialization of its members. The presumptuous attempt at establishing a normative standard for human cognition, emotion, and behavior was questionable at best for obvious reasons. The philosophical basis of this body of theory and practice, which claims to explain and understand "human nature," is not authentic or applicable to all human groups (Nobles, 1986). White (1972), in his article "Towards a Black Psychology," speaks to this issue clearly when he contends that "it is difficult if not impossible to understand the lifestyles of Black people using traditional psychological theories, developed by white psychologists to explain white behavior." White further asserts that when these theories are applied to different populations, many weakness-dominated and inferiority-oriented conclusions are uncovered. One has only to examine the psychological literature as it relates to Black people to appreciate White's point.

HISTORICAL THEMES IN PSYCHOLOGICAL RESEARCH

Historically, research on minorities in general and on Blacks in particular has shifted focus several times. For example, the Black family has been the object of study for over three hundred years, and the source of some very controversial hypotheses. The assumptions of those who sought to paint the Black family as the picture of disorganization and pathology (Frazier, 1939; Moynihan, 1965; Rainwater, 1966) underwent challenges from those whose views of the Black family were more positive, culturally congruent, and functional (Billingsley, 1968; Ladner, 1971; Nobles, 1978; McAdoo, 1981). In fact, Thomas and Sillen (1972) and Sue (1978) concluded that it is difficult to fully understand and appreciate the status of ethnic minority research without reference to several general themes or models. These models include:

1. The inferiority model.
2. The deprivations/deficit model
3. The multicultural model.

Figure 1.1 provides a conceptual outline of these research trends, and a brief review follows.

FIGURE 1.1 Historical Themes in Black Psychological Research.

	INFERIORITY	DEFICIT/DEFICIENCY	MULTICULTURAL
Definition	Blacks are intellectually, physically, and mentally inferior to whites,	Blacks deficient with respect to intelligence, cognitive styles, family structure.	All culturally distinct groups have strengths and limitations.
Etiology of Problem	Genetics/heredity, individual.	Lack of proper environmental stimulation; racism and oppressive conditions, individual.	Differences viewed as different; lack of skills needed to assimilate.
Relevant Hypothesis and Theories	Genetic inferiority, eugenics.	Cultural deprivation, cultural enrichment.	
Research Examples	White (1799) Morton (1839) Jensen (1969)	Moynihan (1965) Kardiner and Ovesey (1951)	J. White (1972) Nobles (1972, 1981) Sue (1981)

INFERIORITY MODELS

The inferiority model generally contends that Black people are inferior to Whites. Its focus is sharpened by the theories of genetics and heredity, which contend that the development of the human species is determined by heredity and views this process of development as "in the blood" or encoded in the genes. This model apparently afforded for some a scientific basis for viewing Blacks as inferior. Examples of these assertions of racial inferiority, as reported by Clark (1975), were heard as early as 1799 when Professor Charles White spoke of the negro as being "just above the ape in the hierarchy of animal/human development, having a small brain, deformed features, an ape-like odor, and an animal immunity to pain." These inferiority assertions continued into the mid-1800s when studies on cranial capacities showed that a European skull held more pepper seed than an African skull, and thus led to the conclusion that Blacks have inferior brains and limited capacity for mental growth (Clark, 1975).

These assertions of racial inferiority continued well into the 1900s, and were promoted by many leading Euro-American psychologists. In fact, a comprehensive examination of the literature related to the history and systems of psychology would reveal that, in all decades encompassing 1900–1970, prominent American psychologists (many of whom were presidents of the American Psychological Association) were proponents of the genetic inferiority hypothesis (Guthrie, 1976). While such facts may be new information for many students in psychology, certainly most students and lay persons are aware of the well publicized assertions of racial and intellectual inferiority by Arthur Jensen (1969).

DEPRIVATION/DEFICIENCY MODEL

The deprivation/deficiency model began to emerge around the late 1950s to early 1960s, and suggested that Blacks are somehow deficient with respect to intelligence, perceptual skills, cognitive styles, family structure, and other factors. Unlike the inferiority model, the set of hypotheses suggested that environmental rather than hereditary factors were responsible for the presumed deficiencies in Blacks. The deficit model arose in opposition to the inferiority model and was formed by more liberal-minded psychological and educational researchers who sought to place on society the burden for Black people's presumed mental and intellectual deficiencies. For example, it was somehow concluded that the effects of years of racism and discrimination had deprived most Black people of the strengths to develop healthy self-esteem (Kardiner and Ovessey, 1951), as well as legitimate family structures (Moynihan, 1965). From this deficit model came such hypotheses as "cultural deprivation," which presumed that, due to the inadequate exposure to Euro-American values, norms, customs and lifestyles, Blacks were indeed "culturally deprived" and required cultural enrichment.

Implicit in the concept of cultural deprivation, however, is the notion that the dominant White middle-class culture established *the* normative standard. Thus, any behaviors, values, and lifestyles that differed from the Euro-American norm were seen as deficient.

By and large, the model of the Black family that has received the most attention has been the deficit-deficiency model. This model begins with the historical assumption that there was no carry-over from Africa to America of any sophisticated African-based form of family life in communal living. The assumption further indicates that viable patterns of family life either did not exist because Africans were incapable of creating them, or they were destroyed beginning with slavery in the separation of biological parents and children, forced breeding, the slave master's sexual exploitation of Black women, and the cumulative effects of three hundred years of socio-economic discrimination. The deficit-deficiency model assumes that, as a result of this background of servitude, deprivation, second-class citizenship, and chronic unemployment, Black adults have not been able to develop marketable skills, self-sufficiency, future orientation, planning and decision-making competencies, and instrumental behaviors thought to be necessary for sustaining a successful two-parent nuclear family while guiding children through the socialization process.

A variation of the deficit-deficiency model was the Black matriarchy model. In a society that placed a premium on decisive male leadership in the family, the Black male was portrayed as lacking the masculine sex role behaviors characterized by logical thinking, willingness to take responsibility for others, assertiveness, managerial skills, achievement orientation, and occupational mastery. In contrast, the Black female was portrayed by this model as a matriarch who initially received her power because society was unwilling to permit the Black male to assume the legal, economic, and social positions necessary to become a dominant force within the family and community life. Having achieved this power by default, the Black female was portrayed as being unwilling to share it. Her unwillingness to share her power was presumed to persist even when the Black male was present and willing to assume responsibility in the family circle, since she was not confident of the male's ability to follow through on his commitments. Confrontation over decision making and family direction was usually not necessary because the Black male was either not present in the household on any ongoing basis, or he was regarded as ineffective by the female when he was present.

MULTICULTURAL MODEL

The rise in the multicultural model has been stimulated by the contention that behaviors, life styles, languages, etc., can only be judged as appropriate or inappropriate within a specific cultural context (Grier & Cobbs, 1968; White, 1972; Pedersen, 1982). The multicultural model assumes and recognizes that each culture has strengths and limitations, and, rather than being viewed as deficient, differences between ethnic groups are viewed as simply different. While the multicultural model is the latest trend in research with respect to minorities in general and Blacks in particular, and is certainly a more positive approach to research with culturally distinct groups, it is by no means immune to the conceptual and methodological flaws that have plagued psychological research efforts both past and present.

   In some respects, this new emphasis of ethnic pluralism has helped researchers to focus on culture-specific models in a multicultural context. Black psychology has been the forerunner of an ethnic and cultural awareness in psychology that has worked its way into the literature on child development, self-image, family dynamics, education, communication patterns, counseling and psychotherapy, and mental health delivery systems. The blossoming of Black psychology has been followed by the assertion on the part of Asian American psychologists (Sue and Wagner, 1973; Sue, 1981), Chicano psychologists (Martinez, 1977), and Native American psychologists (Richardson, 1981) that sociocultural differences in the experiential field must be considered as legitimate correlates of behavior. The development of an ethnic dimension in psychology suggested that other non-White Americans wanted to take the lead in defining themselves rather than continuing the process of being defined by the deficit-deficiency models of the majority culture. The evolution of the ethnic cultural perspective enlarged the scope of psychology.

It served as a corrective step that reduced psychology's reliance on obsolete and inaccurate stereotypes in defining culturally distinct people.

BLACK BEHAVIORAL NORMS

Given the negativistic conceptions of Black people and Black behavior that emerged from the Euro-American frame of reference, it was clear that an alternate frame of reference was not only appropriate, but absolutely necessary. An interesting debate (Nobles, 1986) is whether one considers the awarding of Sumner's degree in 1920, the establishment of the Association of Black Psychologists in 1968, or the era in Ancient KMT as the marker for the establishment of the discipline of Black psychology. What is undebatable, however, is the recognition that general psychology had failed to provide a full and accurate understanding of the Black reality. As such, the discipline of Black psychology and the new emergence of an African psychological perspective can be defined as a discipline of science (continuing to evolve), which is attempting to study, analyze, and define appropriate and inappropriate behaviors of Black and African people from an Afro-centric frame of reference.

A second point made by White (1972) in his article is that Black psychology as a discipline should emerge out of the authentic experiences of Blacks in America. On the surface, White's contention seems absolutely logical. However, we believe this premise requires closer scrutiny.

For years, Black psychologists in the discipline of Black psychology have concerned themselves with trying to combat negativistic assumptions made about Black people by White society in general and traditional psychology in particular. In doing so, many of the writings have been reactionary in their attempts to combat the racist and stereotypic assumptions perpetuated by the Euro-American culture. In that regard, Black psychology has served a vital purpose in the evolution of thought about the psychology of African-American people. In their attempt to negate the White, middle-class norm, and to assert the necessity for analyzing African-American behavior in the context of its own norms, Black psychologists have been attempting to establish this uniquely Afrocentric normative base. In developing that norm, however, new questions are now being raised about whether or not the behavior of Black people in America constitutes a reasonable normative standard of what appropriate and/or inappropriate behavior should be. In fact, if one examines the research related to Blacks, the "normative" standard emerged for the most part from the analysis of behaviors and attitudes of Southern-born, working-class, ghetto-dwelling Black people (Akbar, 1981).

While this norm was certainly more valid than the Euro-centric perspective, it introduced biases against large numbers of Blacks who did not fit the newly developed stereotype of what a "real" Black person should be. Figure 1.2 attempts to illustrate how ghetto-centric norms are indeed based on a relatively small sample of Black people, and are influenced by a Euro-centric perspective of what Black normative behavior should be.

One can readily see the problem in adapting this ghetto-centric norm to all Black people in the criticism that is being leveled at TV's "The Cosby Show." Much of the negative press about the show from the Black community has to do with the assumption that the characters and/or the show itself are not "Black enough." Many assume (inappropriately) that you cannot be Black and middle-class, have two working professional parents, and be a member of a loving family who displays caring concern, strength, and character, all in a single episode.

Apparently, many Black psychologists are now recognizing the difficulty that this shortsighted perspective has created

FIGURE 1.2. Need for a World View That Emerges from an African Frame of Reference.

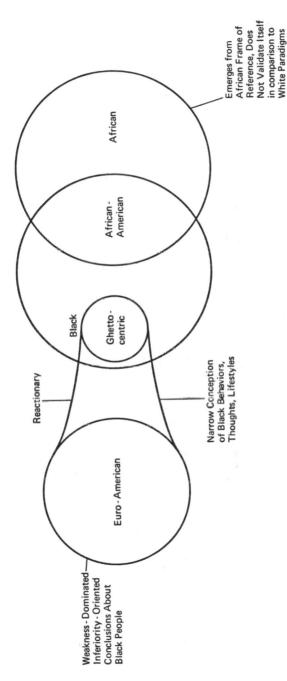

13

for Black people. Akbar (1981) has suggested that this "Black norm" has two major limitations. First, it validates itself in comparison to a White norm. Secondly, the norm assumes that the adaptation to the conditions of America by Blacks constitutes a reasonable normative statement about African-American behavior. Akbar (1981) had the unique vision to recognize that oppression, discrimination, and racism are unnatural human phenomena; as such, these conditions stimulate unnatural human behavior. Thus, many of the behaviors displayed by Blacks, as they attempt to adjust and react to hostile conditions in America, may be functional but often prove self-destructive. For example, one who perceives her or his employment options as limited or nonexistent (because of discrimination) may turn to a life of crime in order to provide her- or himself with what are perceived as basic necessities. Such an individual might be seen selling drugs for profit, burglarizing a local establishment, engaging in prostitution or pimping, or other illegitimate endeavors. The problem with the ghetto-centric norm is that it legitimizes such behavior.

Because of these questions, many psychologists are now suggesting that statements about normative behavior should emerge from the values, norms, customs, and philosophies that are Afri-centric. The debate about what constitutes normative Black behavior is likely to rage on within the discipline of Black psychology for many years. Readers may ask, however, "What is this Afro-centric norm, and how does it manifest itself in the Black community?" In the first edition of *The Psychology of Blacks*, White (1984) offers an excellent synthesis of the Afri-centric value system.

THE AFRICAN WORLD VIEW

White (1984) views the holistic, humanistic ethos described by Nobles (1972) and Mbiti (1970) as the principal feature of

African psychology. There appears to be a definite correspondence between the African ethos and the Afro-American world view in terms of the focus on emotional vitality, interdependence, collective survival, the oral tradition, perception of time, harmonious blending, and the role of the elderly. Some have questioned the utility of an African normative base, given the enormous tribal and geographical variability among African people. However, to discount the presence of an African norm because of differences is analogous to missing the forest for the trees. Certainly, there are individual differences, but there are more commonalities than differences, and those common themes provide the foundation for the African world view.

The African world view begins with a holistic conception of the human condition. There is no mind-body or affective-cognitive dualism. The human organism is conceived as a totality made up of a series of interlocking systems. This total person is simultaneously a feeling, experiencing, sensualizing, sensing, and knowing human being living in a dynamic, vitalistic world where everything is interrelated and endowed with the supreme force of life. There is a sense of aliveness, intensity, and animation in the music, dance, song, language, and life styles of Africans. Emotions are not labeled as bad; therefore, there is no need to repress feelings of compassion, love, joy, or sensuality.

The basic human unit is the tribe, not the individual. The tribe operates under a set of rules geared toward collective survival. Cooperation is therefore valued above competition and individualism. The concept of alienation is nonexistent in African philosophy since the people are closely interconnected with each other in a way of life that involves concern and responsibility toward others. In a framework that values collective survival, where people are psychologically interdependent on each other, active aggression against another person is in reality an act of aggression against oneself (Nobles, 1976). The idea of interrelatedness extends to the whole universe, arranged in a hierarchy that includes God, humans, animals, plants, and inanimate objects in a descending order.

People are linked together in a geographical and temporal frame by the oral tradition, with messages being transmitted across time and space by word of mouth or the drums. Each tribe contains a griot, an oral historian, who is a living record of the people's heritage. The spoken word is revered. Words take on a quality of life when they are uttered by the speaker. In the act of Nommo the speaker literally breathes life into a word. Nothing exists, including newborn babies, until a name has been uttered with the breath of life. When words are spoken, the listener is expected to acknowledge receiving the message by responding to the speaker. This is known as the call-response. The speaker sends out a message or a call, and the listener makes a response indicating that he or she has heard the message. The speaker and the listener operate within a shared psycholinguistic space affirming each other's presence.

Time is marked off by a series of events that have been shared with others in the past or are occurring in the present. Thus, when an African talks about time in the past tense, reference points are likely to be established by events such as a daughter's marriage or a son's birth, events that were shared with others. When an African is trying to make arrangements about meeting someone in the immediate future, a specific time, such as three o'clock, is avoided. The person is more likely to say, "I will meet you after I finish milking the cows." The primary time frames in African languages are past and present. There is no word in most African languages for the distant future. The distant future has not yet happened; therefore, it does not exist. In this fluid perception of time there is no guilt about wasting time. Time is not a monetary commodity but an experience to be shared with others.

Time is also considered to be repetitive. The major events used to designate points in time, such as conception, birth, the naming ceremony, puberty, and marriage, repeat themselves throughout the life cycle. There is a cyclical, rhythmic pattern to the flow of events—the coming and going of the seasons, the rising and the setting of the sun, and the movement through the stages of life. Nature's rhythms are believed to have been put in order by God, who knew what He was doing. The essence of life is to be able to move harmoniously with the cyclical rhythms of the universe's internal clock. The goal is not to control or dominate the universe, but to blend creatively into the tempo and pace of the seasons of life. Life is broken down into a series of stages beginning with conception, followed by birth, the naming ceremony, puberty, initiation rites, marriage, adulthood, and old age. Death is seen as a stage of life. The living dead are still members of the tribe, and personal immortality is assured as long as one's memory is continuously passed down to each generation by the tribe's oral historian. Since immortality is guaranteed by the passing of one's memory forward, there is no pervasive fear of old age and death. The tribal elders are valued because they have accumulated the wisdom of life's teachings. In the hierarchical arrangement of the cosmos, they occupy a position just below that of the Supreme Being and the living dead.

THE PERSISTENCE
OF THE AFRICAN WORLD VIEW

The African influence persisted in Black life in America because it provided a familiar pattern of customs, folklore, and beliefs about the supernatural and collective survival, allowing the early African-Americans to establish a sense of meaning and direction in the world around them. By holding onto the roots of the African ethos, the slaves and their descendants were able to create a collective psychological space, independent of the oppressor, where they could generate a sense of worth, dignity, and belonging (Gutman, 1976; Fredrickson, 1976).

This collectively shared psychological space served as a protective screen that prevented the slaves from internalizing the oppressor's view of White superiority and Black inferiority. Within this shared psychological space, Blacks have been able to attach completely different cultural meanings to White people's concepts of bad and good. For example, in Afro-American folklore, angry, defiant, fearless Black males who are considered to be extremely undesirable by the White man are held in awe and admiration by members of the Black community because of their determination and facility in dealing with the White establishment.

The remnants of the African tradition within Black culture were handed down from generation to generation by the oral tradition operating within informal and formal communal institutions such as the Black church, extended family networks, fraternal orders, women's clubs, and street corner society. The continuing presence of the African tradition in contemporary Afro-American is exemplified in the Black A.M.E., Baptist, and even Catholic churches. The content is Euro-American, but the style and form shows a definite African influence (Nobles, 1977). In the "git-down" Black Baptist church, for example, where the soul folks righteously take care of business every Sunday morning (and sometimes all afternoon), the content of the service is Euro-American. Black people pray from a Bible written in English, the language of the songs and sermons are in English, or at least what some people might refer to as an Afro-American version of English, but the similarity ends here. Anyone who has observed the joy, spontaneity, call-response language between preacher and congregation, the amen corner, and the close fellowship of the flock has been provided with a visual-auditory demonstration of the continuing presence of an African influence.

Traditional scholars have been unwilling to recognize the presence of an African influence in Black life styles. According to this view, whatever existed in the way of African culture was stamped out by the brutal effects of slavery and the subsequent economic, legal, and political oppression. African-Americans are solely the product of American society. To the extent that differences between Euro-Americans and African-Americans exist, they represent inferior approximations on the part of Black Americans' attempts to imitate Euro-Americans rather than intrinsically different cultural and psychosocial styles. This type of thinking is at the core of the pathology, deficit, deprivation models of Black inferiority.

The revisionists (Blassingame, 1972; Gutman, 1976; Nobles, 1974) who have emerged in recent years take the view that the slaves had cultural and psychological resources of their own, from which emerged the range and complexity of Afro-American life styles we see today. They reject the view that the slaves were only empty vessels who were acted upon, shaped, and dominated by Euro-American society. They do not reject the influence of Euro-American values on Afro-Americans. They view Blackness or Black culture as representing an admixture of two world views coming together, with the African world view as its guiding foundation (Nobles, 1974).

The presence of Afro-American values is not always apparent in the public behavior of brothers and sisters. Some Blacks, typified by Nathan Hare's *Black Anglo Saxon* (1965) and E. Franklin Frazier's *Black Bourgeoisie* (1962), attempt to deny all traces of Afro-American life styles in their behavior. They consider Euro-American cultural values and expressive styles to be superior. In commenting on how the Black race had prospered under the guidance of White folks, Booker T. Washington (1932), one of the leading Black spokespersons at the turn of the century, was reported to have said that folks went into slavery as pagans and came out as Christians, went into slavery without language and came out speaking the beautiful Anglo-Saxon tongue.

In less guarded moments, however, many of these Black Anglo-Saxons show evidence of having internalized definite aspects of the Black culture. Nathan Hare (1965) describes a group of Black classical music majors who were listening to and discussing the finer nuances of the music of Euro-American composers when unbeknownst to them someone put on a blues-and-rhythm tune by a popular Black singer. Despite their denials of having ever heard of this Black performer, the brothers and sisters were soon popping their fingers and dancing in time with the music. Hare's anecdote suggests that all Black Americans have internalized in varying degrees the behaviors, attitudes, and expressive patterns of the Afro-American ethos. Many of us are aware of the brothers who in their daily speech try to affect totally the tone, pace, and diction of standard oral English, yet their whole language demeanor changes when they fall into the "mama you sho' is fine" love rapping designed to get them over with some super fine sister.

At the other end of the Black identity continuum, the remnants of African culture are highly visible in the behavioral pattern and languages of the Geeches who live on the sea islands off the coast of Georgia. These Blacks, whose ancestors were brought to the islands direct from West Africa have been culturally isolated from the main stream of both Black and White America for decades. The sounds and syntax patterns in their speech, as well as the nearly six hundred words used in personal names, nicknames, song, and dances are almost identical to those used in Ibo, Yoruba, Mandingo, and Wolof languages of West Africa (Smitherman, 1977). In a similar fashion, Counter and Evans (1981) have studied and identified similar cultural characteristics in the people of Suriname, who have managed to retain their African cultural heritage and customs after successfully battling the Dutch slave traders for their freedom in the 1600s.

One can think of Black Americans as being spread along a cultural spectrum, the majority representing a combination of both African and American culture (Blackness) somewhere between the Geeches who show almost pure Africanism in their behavior at one extreme and the Black Anglo-Saxons who attempt to deny any traces of the African ethos at the other.

THE DEVELOPMENT OF BLACK PSYCHOLOGY: THE MODERN ERA

The modern era of Black psychologists begins in 1968 with the formation of the Association of Black Psychologists (ABPSI). Graduate schools in psychology were still turning out a combined national total of only three or four Black Ph.D.'s in psychology a year. Some major departments of psychology at this late date had not produced a single Black Ph.D. psychologist. The grand total of psychologists among the more than ten thousand members of the American Psychological Association (APA), psychology's most prestigious organization, was less than one percent. At the annual convention of APA in San Francisco in September, 1968, approximately fifty-eight Black psychologist delegates and their guests came together to give form and substance to the idea of a national organization of Black psychologists.

The group of Black psychologists who came together knew about the needs, aspirations, and goals of Blacks from direct experience. They had grown up in the oral tradition of the Black community as sons and daughters of working-class, marginally employed and underemployed shoeshine boys, maids, janitors, waiters, beauty operators, numbers runners, nonunion cooks, all-purpose laborers, and jack-leg preachers. Having received their graduate and professional training in the traditional theories of psychology, they were well aware of the flaws in the White person's logic when it came to offering deficit-oriented psychological explanations about the behavior of Blacks. With their combination of direct experience obtained by growing up in the Black community and academic training in the basic models of psychology, these Black psychologists were uniquely qualified to formulate the theoretical principles and applied direction of Black psychology. They did not discover Black psychology. Black psychology is as old as African heritage and the cultural complexion Blacks have sustained within the American society. The job of Black psychologists was and is to articulate in psychological terms what was already present in the Black experience.

Finally, Black psychologists adopted a posture of social and political advocacy. Our White colleagues in psychology maintained that they were objective scientists whose research findings were politically neutral. Yet, somehow their findings, which were used to formulate public policies such as benign neglect and compensatory education, defined Black people from a point of view that concentrated on defectiveness and pathology. Black psychologists have been honest from the beginning, "we are pro-Black," actively interested in the psychological well-being of Blacks, and willing to speak out against those social programs, research paradigms, and theoretical formulations that have a potentially oppressive effect on Blacks. At the same time, have striven to implement the psychological models and social programs that they feel will improve the quality of life in the Black community.

In the twenty-one years since its formal beginning in 1968, the modern era of Black psychology has established its presence across several areas of psychology. The impact of the efforts of Black psychologists have been felt in the areas of community mental health, education, intelligence and ability testing, professional training, forensic psychology, and criminal justice. Black psychologists have presented their findings at professional conferences, legislative hearings, and social policy-making task forces; they have served as expert witnesses in class action suits designed to make institutional policy more responsive to the needs of Black people. In light of the social phenomenon and institutional policies that continue to affect the mental health needs of the Black community, we expect the association of Black Psychologists will be a vital and necessary resource for some time to come.

In summary, Black psychology and the psychology of Blackness reflect an attempt to build a conceptual model that organizes, explains, and leads to understanding the psychosocial behavior of African-Americans based on the primary dimensions of an African-American world view. While the necessity for its development goes almost without question, perhaps not so clear-cut is the fact that the major forces that stimulated the growth of the contemporary Black psychology movement were the failure of general psychology to provide a full and accurate understanding of Black reality and the dehumanization of Black people resulting from applications of Euro-centric norms.

CHAPTER TWO

THE BLACK FAMILY[1]

The attempt to synthesize the enormous amount of research on Black families will be difficult at best. Doing so, however, requires that we review a framework for categorizing the research, as well as some of the problems and difficulties that have plagued previous research efforts.

HISTORICAL VIEWS

Myers (1982) suggests that the research and literature on the Black family can be understood in the context of several themes. He has identified five distinct emphases and related hypotheses, which serve as underlying themes for different segments of research. The themes include:

- *Poverty-acculturation:* The research suggests that Black families were more successful and healthy to the degree that they emulated and assimilated the norms and values of the White middle class.
- *Pathology:* This theme is built on the principles of the Black matriarchy, emphasizing the consequences of poverty. The research in this area provided supposed empirical evidence for the disorganized family, which contributed to the presumed personality, social, cognitive, and mental deficits in children.

- *Reactive-apology:* The studies challenged pathology notions and suggested that the Black families under study were similar to those of Whites, except for the fact that they have been subjected to racism, discrimination, poverty, and oppression.

- *Black nationalist:* The research and literature sought to emphasize the strengths and competencies of Black families rather than the deficiencies and pathology. These studies also sought to provide legitimacy and validation for the Black culture, which was said to be unique and distinct from the White European norm.

- *Proactive-revisionist:* Allowing the old questions regarding the Black family to be restated and reconceptualized, the research from this era presented not only a more positive portrayal of Black families, but also a more complex and realistic picture of Black families, which had grounding in empirical research.

CONCEPTUAL PITFALLS

The research efforts represented by several of these themes have also been plagued by several fundamental mistakes.

The first mistake is that researchers in the poverty/acculturation, pathology, and reactive-apology themes attempted to use Euro-American family norms as a standard of comparison for Black families. White (1972) has clearly articulated the inappropriateness of such comparisons by suggesting that it is difficult, if not impossible, to understand the life styles of Black people using traditional theories developed by Whites to explain Whites. Nobles (1984) has also speculated about the motives for making such comparisons and arriving at such negative conclusions by suggesting that those who control the information, control. Nobles contends that the most efficient way to keep Black people oppressed and powerless is to provide society with ideas that justify and certify the inferior status and condition of Black people. Accordingly, the domination and exploitation of Black people are guaranteed by the production of information and ideas legitimizing Black oppression (Nobles, 1984).

For example, when the offspring of matriarchal families met in the next generation as adults, the pathology theme found it difficult to conceive how they could develop a mutually satisfying relationship. The research suggested that the Black male was confused, didn't know who he was, and lacked the emotional maturity required for the on-going responsibility of family living. The Black female was also thought to have an exaggerated sense of her own worth, not to have much confidence in the male's ability to meet his obligations over a prolonged period, and to feel that he had very little preparation for the give-and-take of male-female relationships. It was further assumed by deficit-oriented researchers that putting two people like these, who have been reared in matriarchal families, together in a conjugal union or marriage of their own would only be the beginning of another vicious, destructive, deficit-deficiency cycle with the "tangle and web of pathology" recreating itself.

The proponents of the pathology-oriented, matriarchal family model did not consider the possibility that a single-parent Black mother could serve as an adequate role model for the children of both sexes. The notion that the mother could reflect a balance of the traditional male and female roles, with respect to mental toughness and emotional tenderness, was largely ignored because of the rigid classification of psychosexual roles in American society. In the Black community, however, the categorization of social role behaviors based on gender is not as inflexible. It is conceivable that a Black mother could project a combination of assertive and nurturant behaviors in the process of rearing children of both sexes as nonsexist adults.

With the reality of accelerating divorce rates, in recent years the single-parent family headed by a woman has become a social reality in Euro-America. This reality has been accompanied by an attempt on the part of social scientists to legitimize family structures that represent alternatives to the nuclear family while reconceptualizing the social roles of males and females with less emphasis on exclusive behaviors. The concept of androgyny has been introduced to cover the vast pool of human personality traits that can be developed by either sex (Rogers, 1978). In contemporary times, a well-balanced person reflects a combination of both instrumental and expressive traits. The latter include feeling-oriented behaviors formerly considered feminine, such as tenderness, caring, and affection. The former includes characteristics that help the family to survive and meet its basic needs for shelter, food, clothing, wellness, and safety, using economic resources. Thus, it is conceptually possible for a White, single, and androgynous female parent to rear psychologically healthy, emotionally integrated children. It is interesting how the sociology of the times makes available to White Americans psychological concepts designed to legitimize changes in the family, in child-rearing patterns, and in relationships between the sexes. Yet these same behaviors, when first expressed by Afro-Americans, were considered pathological. For example, what White psychologists considered to be a "tangle and web of pathology" and a disorganized family system in Black female-headed households is now renamed "single-parent families" because such phenomena are now being observed in White families.

A second fundamental mistake is that selected researchers from every period have attempted to characterize the Black family as a single entity (nuclear versus extended) and inferred that all Black families should be viewed as such. Adherence to any one model as a norm for all Blacks may be inappropriate because it inevitably, albeit unintentionally, excludes smaller segments of the Black community. This notion of a dynamic, flexible, changing Black family is also amplified in the writings of Jewell (1988), who views the Black family as an entity that changes in order to meet its needs during a given life cycle. To support her assertion, Jewell cites examples of how, during the last two and one-half decades, the number of Black families headed by husbands and wives in 1960 (74 percent) has decreased (55 percent in 1980), while the number of female-headed households in the 1960s (22 percent) has increased to 41 percent during this same period. Jewell also reminds us, as do Billingsley (1968) and Hill (1971), that changes in the structures of Black families are often precipitated by changing economic fortunes and/or circumstances.

Despite the fact that his writings are two decades old, Billingsley (1968) ably illustrated this point by proposing that, during a particular life cycle, the Black family could take any one of three basic forms:

1. *Nuclear:* Related family members only
2. *Extended:* Other relatives living with family
3. *Augmented:* Nonrelated friends living with family

These three forms had three different dimensions:

1. *Incipient:* No children
2. *Simple:* Children
3. *Attenuated:* Single parent

Thus, there were twelve possible variations:

1. *Nuclear-incipient:* Husband and wife in the home, no children, no relatives or others
2. *Nuclear-simple:* Husband and wife in the home, children present, no relatives or others
3. *Nuclear-attenuated:* Single parent, children present, no relatives or others
4. *Extended-incipient:* Husband and wife, no children present, other relatives in the home
5. *Extended-simple:* Husband and wife, children present, other relatives also present
6. *Extended-attenuated:* Single parent, children present, other relatives also present
7. *Augmented-incipient:* Husband and wife present, no children, non-relatives in the home

8. *Augmented-incipient-extended:* Husband and wife present, relatives and nonrelatives in the home
9. *Augmented-nuclear:* Husband and wife present, children present, nonrelatives also living in the home
10. *Augmented-nuclear-extended:* Husband and wife present, children present, relatives and nonrelatives living in the home
11. *Augmented-attenuated:* Single parent, children present, nonrelatives living in the home
12. *Augmented-attenuated-extended:* Single parent, children present, relatives and nonrelatives living in the home

For a more extensive discussion of family variations, readers should consult Billingsley's *Black Families in White America* (1968, pp. 15–21).

THE EXTENDED FAMILY MODEL

The extended family, in contrast to the single-parent, subnuclear family, consists of a related and quasi-related group of adults, including aunts, uncles, parents, cousins, grandparents, boyfriends, and girlfriends linked together in a kinship or kinlike network. They form a cooperative interface with each other, confronting the concerns of living and rearing children. This model of family life—which seems able to capture not only the strength, vitality, resilience, and continuity of the Black family, but also the essence of Black values, folkways, and life styles—begins with a different set of assumptions about the development and evolution of Black family life in America.

The Black extended family is seen as an outgrowth of African patterns of family and community life that survived in America. The Africans carried with them, through the mid-Atlantic passage and sale to the initial slave owners, a well developed pattern of kinship, exogenous mating, and communal values, emphasizing collective survival, mutual aid, cooperation, mutual solidarity, interdependence, and responsibility for others (Nobles, 1974; Blassingame, 1972). These values became the basis for the Black extended family in America. They were retained because they were familiar and they allowed the slaves to have some power over destiny by enabling them to develop their own styles for family interaction. A consciousness of closeness to others, belongingness, and togetherness protected the slaves from being psychologically destroyed by feelings of despair and alienation, and the extended family provided a vehicle to pass the heritage on to the children (Frederickson, 1976; Gutman, 1976).

The Black extended family, with its grandparents, biological parents, conjugal partners, and other relatives, is an intergenerational group. The members of this multigenerational family do not necessarily reside in the same household. Individual households are part of a social-familial network that functions like a minicommunity. The members band together to share information, resources, and communal concerns (Stacks, 1974). There is no central authority—matriarchal or patriarchal. Decisions are made on an equalitarian model with input and outcomes determined by who is available at a given time, who has expertise with reference to a given problem, and who has prior experience and a track record in decision making. This is likely to give some edge to family elders. They are looked up to within the extended family network as resource people and advisors because they have the life experience that is highly valued in the Black community. As in the past, the family has held together over time and geographical space by a shared experience frame and a common set of values.

ALTERNATE CONCEPTUALIZATIONS

Obviously, any attempt to conceptualize the Black family must consider these possible variations in family structure, as well as the influence of other variables, such as social class based on socio-economic status, on the structure of Black families.

Our reactions, as well as those of other Black researchers, to the negative descriptions of the Black family have been intended to object to the conclusions reached by Euro-American scholars regarding the supposed pathology in the Black family. While our reactions have succeeded in serving as a critique of poor scholarship, by implication, some of our reactions have also clouded the fact that a specific phenomenon observed exists in reality. The result is that many of us in the Black community ignore social pathology in our families and communities, believing instead that "since White folks said it, it must not be true." Consequently, we exert little effort in trying to address the issues that need correcting.

In essence, we believe that the problem with much of the Black family research is not in the phenomenon being observed, but in the implications and conclusions drawn from the observations. Moynihan (1965) for example, attempted to describe the family as a "tangle and web of pathology." Despite the fact that Moynihan's conclusions, assumptions, and methodology were questionable, inaccurate, and in some cases inappropriate, the observations that too many single women are heading Black families, that some families lack male leadership and support, that some children lack suffient role modeling, and that some Black males and females are struggling to get along are issues in need of attention. Logically, then, the challenge presented to contemporary researchers interested in the Black family is to follow the lead of the researchers who represent the proactive-revisionist trend of Black family research (i.e., Wade Nobles, Harriett McAdoo), and continue to restate old questions and reconceptualize family dynamics in ways that are more consistent with an Afri-centric cultural heritage. Certainly Billingsley (1968) and others have been successful at reconceptualizing and restating questions and issues on the Black family.

The importance of Black family models and conceptual paradigms (i.e., Billingsley), however, has little or nothing to do with developing a conceptual system merely for classification. The real merit of any classification scheme on the Black family is in its utility for examining family dynamics, not just family composition. Essentially, the real question is how do instrumental and expressive roles manifest themselves within the different family variations when needs have to be met? Also, how do changes in family composition impact the family system's ability to meet those needs? Borrowing from the works of Billingsley (1968) and Mbiti (1970), Mitchell (1989) for example, is developing a five-generation model for continuity and enhancement in the Black family. The five generations reflected in Mitchell's model include unborns, children, adults, elders, and spirits. Mitchell also outlines the important roles played by each generation, and he describes their needs, which must be met by the family system. For example, unborns are important in that they represent a reaffirmation of life, as well as some cultural continuity into the next generation. Their needs include care and protection related to prenatal care for mothers, as well as planning for meeting their instrumental and expressive needs in the future. Children are important in that they provide rewards of parenthood, are extensions of two adults' physical and emotional love, and, through their presence, assure the immortality of their parents. Their needs include care and protection (from the larger society, from others, and themselves), affective development (formal schooling, culture-specific education), and preparation for a dual existence (development of effective responses to realities in both an Afri-centric and Euro-centric environment). Mitchell concludes by arguing that each family unit must assess, plan for, and provide ways to meet the instrumental and expressive needs of its members, regardless of family variation.

Any attempt to understand today's Black family must also involve a recognition of the role of social forces and public policies. We believe that Black families are disproportionately affected by social policies made at every level of government. The situation for many families, particularly those of working or low socio-economic status (SES), is analogous to being caught between a rock and a hard place, in that the policies and programs designed to assist with basic family needs are sometimes a hindrance and a barrier for other families who find them restrictive, misdirected, and just plain unresponsive.

Moore (1981) helps to crystalize this picture in her discussion of Black families affected by social policies. Unemployment rates among Blacks (both adults and youth) are usually among the highest in the nation, and typically twice the average for Whites. Yet many of the community-based job development programs have Blacks disproportionately represented in those courses geared towards low-wage, low-demand occupations, with little, if any, upward mobility. When work can be found, many Blacks find themselves trapped in jobs where income and wages are too low to raise them out of poverty, and yet these meager earnings are too high to qualify them for public assistance.

Rising costs and inflation rates often require both parents or all adult members of a household to be out of the house earning income to support the family. Such situations often leave children without day care or adequate adult supervision for significant periods. When day care facilities are found, they are often too costly and, as such, unusable. Thus, adequate child care is restricted to economically advantaged families who can afford them or to extremely poor families who can receive federal, state, or municipal subsidies.

Many Blacks must also live in impoverished neighborhoods under the poorest of conditions (i.e., unsafe housing,
malnutrition, poverty), which make them more susceptible to
illnesses and diseases than other family groups. Black children
in particular are affected by these conditions, since many
receive inadequate prenatal care prior to birth, are born into
the world prematurely and with low birth weights, have high
infant mortality rates, are affected by mental retardation, and
suffer from malnutrition (National Center for Health Statistics, 1979). Too many children go for long periods (years in
some cases) without any care or checkups by a physician, do
not receive adequate innoculations against childhood diseases, have greater incidences of hypertension and cancer, and
have low life expectancy when compared to any other ethnic
group in the United States. While programs to address the
health concerns of Blacks have been created, they too are prone
to restrictive eligibilities and misapplications that limit their
effectiveness.

FAMILY VALUE SYSTEMS:
AN AFRI-CENTRIC PERSPECTIVE

Our observations of the Black family over several decades
leads us to believe that families differ less in structure and
more in context, functions, and processes involving the trans-
mission of culture, goals, values, roles, and norms. Structur-
ally, most families (Black, White, Hispanic, Asian) have
parents and children who share a common living space. Some
have relatives who live in the home, while others absorb
nonrelated friends into the family system. The fact that some
families consist of one or two parents, as well as several or no
children, often depends on factors that are unrelated to the
cultural prerequisites for family. They are often influenced
more by environmental conditions (such as economics) and

one's ability to adapt to those conditions. Because one observes that a certain percentage of Black families are headed by single parents does not mean that the single-parent family becomes a cultural norm.

Contextually, the fact that more Black families (than White) exist under conditions of poverty and oppression is a reality shared by many in the Black community. Black families must strive to accomplish tasks of child rearing, schooling, providing for basic necessities, and maintaining one's spirituality with less resources than other family groups have. Yet, despite the fact that most are successful at negotiating their way through the obstacles of oppression and discrimination, one should be careful about viewing the impoverished Black family as a cultural norm. On the contrary, one must look beyond the surface structure (family composition) to identify the underlying cultural imperatives.

Sudarkasa (1981) helps us to examine the underlying propositions in identifying the African heritage in African-American families. The author correctly points out that the family kinship was composed of groups of related family members, both those in the bloodline (consanguineous) as well as those who joined the family by marriage (conjugal). In essence, "the family" can consist of a single household where members of two, three, and sometimes four generations occupy a common space; or the family can consist of many individual conjugal units who reside in separate dwellings, where each is tied to the larger family unit through direct blood relations by one of its members. The latter point is an important one in that, rather than being viewed as distinct nuclear family units (a practice endorsed by many Euro-centric researchers), all are considered as part of one family system.

McAdoo (1981) is also clear in her assertions that, while there may be few direct one-to-one carryovers from Africa, the common patterns in family practices between traditional African and contemporary African-American families make it impossible to dismiss the cultural continuity. Given this emphasis on family, the values of innerconnectedness, mutual aid, responsibility, and cooperation can be seen in the daily operations of African-American families in the U.S. For example, decision making in many family systems still centers in the consanguineal core group, particularly as decisions affect the entire family. Authority resides in the elders of the group, usually the oldest male, where brothers, uncles, and other males of that generation serve as an extension of the tribal elders found in African society, in forming a decision-making body (Sudarkasa, 1981). In absence of that male figure, the eldest female usually holds that position in recognition that age rather than gender is the prerequisite for wisdom. Child rearing and socialization were practices shared by the extended family, even though each conjugal family maintained individual responsibility. These practices are readily seen in Black families where extended relatives and significant others provide learning, support, encouragement, and even discipline to young children. For example, if caught doing something wrong, a child could expect to be reprimanded by his or her parents, as well as by aunts, uncles, grandparents, and other family friends who recognize inappropriate behavior as a violation of family expectations for proper conduct.

Another important point made by Sudarkasa (1981) is the recognition that, in Africa, the stability of the extended family was not dependent on the survival of conjugal unions, since the consanguineal ties were the most salient and influential. This point should be emphasized as African-Americans try to interpret the consequences of rising divorce rates and out-of-wedlock childbearing on the viability of contemporary Black families. There is little doubt that these phenomena seriously impact the individual family units. However, since many traditions, values, support systems, and cultural imperatives

are tied to consanguineal connections, the functioning effi-
ciency of the family as a whole may not be impacted as
seriously.

SUMMARY

Many researchers on Black families have been successful in
showing how Black families have perservered and triumphed
through years of oppression and adversity. Undoubtedly, the
characteristics that have helped them to survive are those
related to the African ethos. Therefore, we believe that the
contemporary Black family in America, despite its variations,
is an extension of many African traditions.

Fundamentally, the family rather than the individual is
at the center of one's universe—the point around which all
else revolves. The African ethos of a holistic self in which one's
individual self is perceived only in relation to the tribe or
group is paramount. The family is held together by a set of
common values involving interdependence, mutual aid, resilience, communalism, and collective responsibilities (Nobles,
1978); hence the connectedness to other persons in the extended family network. These values transcend gender roles
and allow both men and women to participate in and contribute to the management of economic resources, child rearing,
community activism, and other issues of family life without
being categorically restricted on the basis of gender. The fluid
distinction between social sex roles offers both men and
women in the Black family network the opportunity to emerge
as decision makers, influence molders, and household managers.

It could be argued that the Black extended family exists
and persists primarily because Black people faced the common fate of oppressive economic and social conditions, and

that it exists out of necessity as a way of surviving an oppressive class system. It would follow from this argument that the Black extended family would disappear as Black people moved up the socio-economic ladder. Yet the extended family does not seem to be disappearing with rising economic fortunes. McAdoo's (1979) work with upwardly mobile and upper middle-class Black families suggests that not only does the extended family model persist when Blacks move up the socio-economic ladder, but the Afro-American values of mutual aid, interdependence, and interconnectedness also remain as the guiding ethos of family existence.

Ultimately, we believe the measure of a family's stability is its resourcefulness, that is, its ability to adapt to environmental realities and challenges in ways that help the family unit meet its needs. Our belief is consistent with the position taken by Hill (1971) who suggested that Black families utilize specific strengths in attempting to meet the needs of its members. Among other African-American researchers of the Black family, there is virtually unanimous agreement that the characteristics that help Black families to develop, survive, and improve are consistent with Hill's (1971) analysis of Black family strengths. These include strong kinship bonds, strong work orientation, strong achievement orientation, adaptability of family roles, and a strong religious orientation.

CHAPTER THREE

THE STRUGGLE FOR IDENTITY CONGRUENCE IN AFRICAN AMERICANS

Questions about the identity development of African-Americans were raised with renewed interest during the seventies and eighties. This renewed interest in the topic has introduced different perspectives on the identity development question, which unfortunately has produced contradictory conclusions. The charge of contemporary researchers, like the focus of this chapter, is to analyze and explain these conceptual contradictions.

IDENTITY AS AN AFRICAN-AMERICAN

By some accounts, identity is defined as one component of an individual's overall self-concept. It involves the adoption of certain personal attitudes, feelings, characteristics, and behaviors (personal identity) and the identification with a larger group of people who share those characteristics (reference group orientation).

Some researchers depicted the African-American's personality and identity as reflecting a pathological adaptation to White American society's racism resulting in low self-esteem and a heightened sense of self-hatred (Kardiner and Ovessy, 1951; Karon, 1975). Another body of research has suggested that, in the context of considerable social oppression, the African-American personality and consciousness evolved through a transformative process in which Blacks struggle to move away from "oppressor identification" and move towards ethnic pride and internalization of positive racial attitudes (Cross, 1971; Thomas, 1971; Jackson, 1976). Still another group of researchers, rejecting the previous theses and hypotheses, state that Black personality is in fact Afro-centrically based (Nobles, 1976, 1980, 1986; Williams, 1981; Akbar, 1981), with an "African self-consciousness" (Baldwin, 1981) serving as the core for the personality system.

For the record, we should state our emphatic rejection of the Black self-hatred thesis which dominated the psychological literature from the early 1940s through the 1950s (Clark & Clark, 1947; Kardiner and Ovessy, 1951). Clearly, the authors of these research articles and manuscripts may have been perceptive in their analysis that White America provided no positive images through which Blacks could see themselves reflected in a positive way. However, the inaccuracy and arrogance of their analysis lie in assuming that Black people look to Whites and to White America as their only source of validation and emulation. Such a perspective completely ignores the necessity (and indeed the cultural imperative) of African-American people to use themselves, their culture, and their history as primary referents. We believe, however, that the latter two bodies of research may have some merit in explaining identity development.

It is our belief that the personality, consciousness, and the core identity of Black people are African in nature. Whether conscious or unconscious, the personality manifests itself in the attitudes, feelings, behaviors, and spiritual essence of African-Americans. Baldwin (1985) provides a clear articulation of the African-American personality in his theory of "African self-consciousness." He writes:

> The core component of the Black personality represents the conscious level expression of the 'oneness of being' communal phenomenology which characterizes the fundamental self-extension orientation of African people. According to Baldwin, while the African self-consciousness system is partly biogenetically determined, and it is also subject to social and environmental influences as well. When this core system of the Black personality is nurtured developmentally as well as situationally through indigenous personal and institutional support systems, it achieves vigorous and full expression in terms of a congruent pattern of basic traits (beliefs, attitudes, and behaviors) which affirm African-American life in the authenticity of its African cultural heritage. [Baldwin, 1985]

Despite Baldwin's assertion that normal Black behavior and consciousness are not merely a reaction to adverse environmental elements, his theory clearly recognizes the interaction between individual personality characteristics and the social and environmental influences that help to form and shape the individual personality. Assuming that an African-American male or female is surrounded by positive (Black-oriented) institutional and social support systems throughout their formative years, then the expected consequence would be the development of a normal, healthy Black personality. Such would be characterized by a strong awareness of and identification with African cultural heritage, a strong sense of motivation directed at insuring collective survival of African people and related institutions, and the active resistance of any force (i.e., racism) that threatens the survival and maintenance of one's people and oneself.

Nobles (1986, p. 96) has also outlined the prerequisites for normal human functioning based on a culturally centered identity. The parameters include:

1. A sense of self that is collective or extended.

2. An attitude wherein one understands and respects the sameness in oneself and others.
3. A clear sense of one's spiritual connection to the universe.
4. A sense of mutual responsibility (for other African people).
5. A conscious understanding that human abnormality or deviancy is any act that is in opposition to oneself.

Other writers on the Black experience are quick to remind us, however, that African-American people are not always afforded the luxury of totally surrounding themselves with social and institutional support systems that enhance, promote, and affirm our humanity as African-Americans.

In fact, James Baldwin (1963), a noted Black author, writes that "to be Black and relatively conscious is to be in a constant state of rage almost all the time." His writings imply that Black people face on-going exposure to racist and oppressive conditions in America from a society that neither validates nor cultivates our existence. If Baldwin's analysis is correct (and we suspect it is), than it is entirely likely that the forces influencing the identity development of many African-Americans are mitigated by oppression and racism.

DISCOVERING AND COPING WITH OPPRESSION

Long before the child can verbalize, he or she is aware of the fact that something is fundamentally wrong in the American society, that some pervasive, catastrophic, and oppressive force is preventing African-American people from achieving their goals and participating in the range of opportunities that America provides for its citizens (Baldwin, 1963). The complete impact of this awareness does not come all at once, but falls into place gradually during middle childhood, preadolescence, early adolescence, young adulthood, and later adulthood stages. As a child looks into the mirror image of society reflected in TV, movies, newspaper, and stories about the heros of American history, he or she sees images of Euro-Americans projected with power, courage, competence, beauty, and goodness.

The conclusion that racism is pervasive in the American society has a profound, lasting, and often devastating influence on African-American young people. They may express their disappointment with anger, fear, resentment, or bitterness. This realization cannot help but generate a period of confusion in Black youth, because it forces them to have to deal with the contradictions that have been inherent in American society for over 350 years. On the one hand, the child has heard that America is the land of equal opportunity, liberty, and justice for all, and that all human beings are created equal and endowed by their Creator with certain inalienable rights. Yet the reality of experiences has made the child aware of the fact that this is definitely not the case.

During late adolescence and early adulthood, Black youth, like other American youth, struggle with major decisions about what to do with their lives, where they are going, how they are going to get there, and how to achieve some degree of economic and political power. In seeking to come to grips with these identity-related issues, Black youth cannot completely avoid the reality of the social contradictions inherent in American life. Those who have been protected from the reality of social contradictions are going to come into contact with other Blacks at this stage; they cannot be permanently isolated from the fact of oppression in American life.

Young adults are confronted with a set of dualities defined by being part of, yet apart from, American society, in it but not of it, included at some level and excluded at others. This duality is at the heart of the identity struggle and generates powerful feelings of rage and indignation (White, 1984). The inclusion-exclusion dilemma is further complicated by their exposure to two different value systems, world views, and historical legacies. In *The Souls of Black Folks*, Dubois (1903) spoke of this cultural and historical duality as a kind of two-ness, a double consciousness created by a confluence of African-American and Euro-American, Black and White realities going on inside of that person at the same time.

Each Black adolescent must attempt to set up some workable balance between Afro-American and Euro-American values within his or her own life space. Complete denial of either frame of reference will restrict choices and personal growth, interpersonal relationships, and economic opportunities. If the individual concentrates solely on a life style that emphasizes individualism, competition, emotional insulation, power, dominance, and control, he or she may achieve success at the cost of being alienated from Black peers and elders who value genuiness, mutual aid, and emotional closeness. This individual may also be relegated to a life of confusion and alienation because their attitudes and behaviors are inconsistent with their cultural essence (Akbar, 1981). On the other hand, if the young adult completely ignores the values that will allow progress in the occupational mainstream, he or she will have dramatically reduced the available range of options and the material quality of life associated with these options.

This duality dilemma is reflected in the writings of Samaj (1981), who presented three phases of the Black extended identity. The apparent struggle many Blacks engage in between Euro-centric and Afro-centric polarities is mirrored in "alien," "diffused," and "collective" identities proposed by Samaj. The Aliens consistently demonstrate a Euro-centric world view, are concerned with their own individual needs rather than the collective good, and either denigrate or deny their Africanity. The diffused try to balance the Black and Alien world views, believing that Black is beautiful while understanding that White is power. They are aware that changes are necessary, but have strong doubts that changes are possible. The collective consistently demonstrate an Afro-centric world view, are committed to the collective survival of Black people, and have the potential to stimulate other Black folks to action.

The analysis by Samaj (1981) also illustrates another facet of the identity question, that is, whether identity development is a dynamic or a static process. "Dynamic" implies constant change, while "static" connotes little change over time. Implied in Samaj's model is the notion that identity, as a construct, can be capsulized into discrete categories (i.e., alien, diffuse, collective). His writings, while differing in content and context, parallel the writings of some 1960s researchers, who sought to construct psychological profiles that divided Black people into static categories based on their orientation towards Blackness (McCord, Howard, Friedberg, and Harwood, 1969; Caplan, 1970). For example, McCord et al. (1969) sought to construct categories that distinguished so-called traditional Negroes from Black Militants.

THE PSYCHOLOGY
OF NIGRESCENCE

Obvious limitations of this nonprocess-oriented research are its failure to account for movement within various identity states (stages), and its tendency to adhere to a stereotypic, all-encapsulating view of Black consciousness. If one can assume that the development of identity is a dynamic process, then movement from one set of attitudes or beliefs to another would be an expected outcome. In fact, a cursory look at the history of African-Americans in this country clearly illustrates this phenomenon. Cross, Parham, and Helms (1989), in their comprehensive review of the Black identity development process, remind us that, in light of the obsessive attempts at deracination (the attempt to erase Black consciousness) by White people and White America, it comes as no surprise that within African-American history are accounts of Blacks who, having first been deculturalized, experience revitalization through a process of nigrescence. "Nigrescence" is derived from the French, and means to become Black. Nigrescence models speculate that the identity development process is characterized by movement between various identity states and/or stages (Cross, 1971; Thomas, 1971; Helms, 1984; Parham, 1989). Cross (1971) introduced the description of the "Negro-to-Black" conversion experience by suggesting that the development of a Black person's racial identity is often characterized by his or her movement through four distinct psychological stages: pre-encounter, encounter, immersion-emersion, and internalization.

Pre-encounter: In this stage, the individual is prone to view the world from a White frame of reference. He or she thinks, acts, and behaves in ways that devalue and/or deny his or her Blackness. The person has accepted a deracinated frame of reference, and, because that reference point is usually a White normative standard, he or she develops very pro-White and anti-Black attitudes.

Encounter: This stage is characterized by an individual experiencing one or many significant (shocking) personal and social events that are inconsistent with his or her frame of reference. For example, a Black person who views his/her race as not important and wishes to be viewed and accepted simply as a "human being" is denied access to living in an exclusive neighborhood because of skin color. These encounters successfully shake a person's self-image of non-Black or "be like White" and make them vulnerable to a new interpretation of self in relation to the world.

The encounter stage appears to involve two phases. The first is a realization phase where an individual recognizes that the old frame of reference or world view is inappropriate, and he/she begins to explore aspects of the new identity. The second phase (decision) occurs when the person—first cautiously, then definitely—decides to develop a Black identity.

Immersion-emersion: This stage represents a turning point in the conversion from the old to the new frame of reference. The period of transition is characterized by a struggle to repress or destroy all vestiges of the pre-encounter orientation while simultaneously becoming intensely concerned with personal implications of the newfound Black identity (Cross, 1978). The person begins to immerse him- or herself into total Blackness, clinging to various elements of the Black culture while simultaneously withdrawing from interactions from other ethnic groups. While the degree of overt manifestations of Blackness are high (i.e., Black clothes and hairstyles, attendance at all Black functions, linguistic style, etc.), the degree of internalized security about one's Blackness is minimal. At this stage, everything of value in life must be Black or relevant to Blackness. This stage is also characterized by a tendency to denigrate White people while simultaneously glorifying Black people (pro-Black/anti-White attitudes).

Internalization: This stage is characterized by the individual's achieving a sense of inner security and self-confidence with his or her Blackness. The resolution of conflicts between the old and new world views becomes evident as tension, emotionality, and defensiveness are replaced by a calm, secure demeanor (Cross, 1978). This stage is also characterized by psychological openness, idealogical flexibility, and a general decline in strong anti-White feelings. While still using Black as a primary reference group, this person moves towards a more pluralistic, nonracist perspective (Cross, 1978).

While the nigrescence models by Cross (1971, 1978) and others (Thomas, 1971; Jackson, 1976; Williams, 1975) are helpful in illustrating both changes in attitude over time, as well as, the within-group variability reflected in the consciousness of African-Americans, they are also prone to limitations. Specifically, these models imply that, while they are process-oriented, their "development-over-time" focus is usually restricted to the late adolescence and early adulthood period in the life cycle.

Consequently, while the stages articulated by Cross document how a person's racial identity can change from one stage to another (i.e., pre-encounter to internalization) during the later adolescent/early adulthood periods, they fail to detail how various stages of racial identity will be accentuated at later stages of life. In an article entitled "Cycles of Psychological Nigrescence," Parham (1989) presents a life cycle nigrescence model based on a modification of the Cross stages. Cross et al. (1989) have noted that the first object of Parham's concern is pinpointing the earliest phase of life at which one is capable of experiencing psychological nigrescence (the process of developing a Black identity). He presupposes that the manifestation of identity during childhood is "more the reflection of parental attitudes or societal stereotypes which a youngster has incorporated" than the integrated, cognitively complex, identity structures found in adults. Consequently, Parham hypothesizes that it is during late adolescence and early adulthood that one might first experience Nigrescence, and thereafter the potential is present for the remainder of one's life. Parham also notes in his writings that there is a qualitative difference between the nigrescence experience at adolescence or early adulthood and the one at middle or late adulthood, because an African-American person's concept of Blackness will be influenced by the distinctive developmental task associated with each phase of adult life. Perhaps the most profound issue Parham raises is not so much that aspects of the initial nigrescence episode vary with age but, once nigrescence is completed, he sees the demand characteristics of each phase of adult development making more likely a person's recycling through the stages. From Parham's perspective, recycling does not mean the person reverts back to the old (pre-encounter) identity and then traverses all the stages. Rather, he is inclined to believe that the challenge or trauma acts as a new encounter episode that exposes small or giant gaps in a person's thinking about Blackness, and the person recycles in order to fill such gaps. Thus depending on the nature of the challenge or the new encounter, recycling may mean anything from a mild refocusing experience, to one involving a full-fledged immersion-emersion episode.

Another important advancement in Parham's (1989) writings is his recognition that a person's initial identity state is not restricted to pre-encounter attitudes. This assertion represents a significant departure from the traditional nigrescence models presented by Cross, Jackson, and Thomas, which implicitly or explicitly suggest that one's racial identity development begins with a pro-White/anti-Black frame of reference or world view. Parham speculates, for example, that if a young adolescent is exposed to and indoctrinated with very pro-Black parental and societal messages, the personal identity and reference group orientation initially developed by that youngster might be pro-Black as well. Contrary to the assumptions implicit in the original nigrescence models, we concur with Akbar (1989) who suggests that the process of identity formation resulting from the positive encounters and affirmations of one's racial identity, rather than that which results from the negative encounter situations experienced in life, are a different and much healthier form of identity development. In fact, Parham (1989) is also clear in his assertion that African-American cultural identity is an entity independent of socially oppressive phenomenon. This independent identity notion provides a critical extension of the original nigrescence theories that initially conceptualized Black identity and the affirmation of oneself as an African-American as only a reaction to the oppressive conditions of White American racism.

A third point of interest in Parham's model is his articulation that identity resolution can occur in at least three ways:

1. *Stagnation:* The failure to move beyond one's initial identity state
2. *Stage-wise linear progression:* Movement from one identity state to another in a sequential, linear fashion
3. *Recycling:* Movement back through the stages once a cycle has already been completed

The Cross (1971), Jackson (1976), and Thomas (1971) models imply that Nigrescence occurs in a linear fashion, with no other alternatives being proposed.

SUMMARY AND CONCLUSIONS

Achieving identity congruence in the face of racist and oppressive elements represents a significant challenge for most African-Americans. Undoubtedly, the achievement of congruence will be facilitated by several important propositions being promoted by contemporary Black psychologists. The first is borrowed from the ancient Africans and simply says "know thyself." Fundamentally, to know oneself (or one's nature) means to recognize, understand, respect, appreciate, and love those characteristics and/or attributes that make us uniquely African-Americans. In addition, self-knowledge helps to dictate behaviors that ultimately support, sustain, and enhance our individual and collective beings as African-Americans. Nobles (1986) asserts that, in knowing one's nature, one is less likely to allow social and environmental conditions to become internalized, and in so doing become the instrument of psychological maladaptation and dysfunction.

The second proposition is borrowed from Baldwin (1986) and Akbar (1981), who suggest that a healthy African self-consciousness is probable if one's personality is nurtured in an environment of supportive personal and institutional systems. In their analysis, a healthy Black psyche is a prescription and a challenge. A *prescription* is a written (in this case) rule or law that outlines the necessary conditions to achieve a purpose or goal (identity congruence). Their prescription suggests the imperative to identify and utilize resources, networks, and institutions within the Black community that affirm and reaffirm our humanity as African-Americans. Our families, schools, churches, social clubs and organizations, and other personal acquaintances must become the instruments by which we maintain congruence in African values, beliefs, and primary sources of validation. The challenge is to recognize our collective responsibility to provide support and nurturance to persons and institutions within the Black community. Recognition of the sameness in ourselves and other African-Americans and self-affirmation are natural outcomes when we extend ourselves to provide support, nurturance, and validation to others. Those who seek validation outside of their "community" will undoubtedly find identity congruence an unachieved goal.

Lastly, Nobles (1986) also reminds us that ideas are the substance of behavior. Consequently, if our consciousness is culturally congruent, then our behavior should be focused on responding to our environmental realities in ways that help to enhance, maintain, and actualize our individual and collective beings as African-Americans. In the African context of being, the self is extended and collective, implying one's connections to others in the community, to those yet unborn, and to those belonging to the community of ancestors. However, it is critical to note, as Myers (1985, p. 35) reminds us, that one's "being" did not automatically make one a part of the community, nor admit one to the position of ancestor at a later date. Both roles required that each adopt a "proper" belief structure as evidenced through attitudes and behaviors.

CHAPTER FOUR

PSYCHOLOGICAL THEMES IN BLACK LANGUAGE, ORAL LITERATURE, AND EXPRESSIVE PATTERNS

INTRODUCTION

Six recurring psychological themes can be identified in the language, oral literature, and expressive patterns of Black folks:

1. Emotional vitality
2. Realness
3. Resilience
4. Interrelatedness
5. The value of direct experience
6. Distrust and deception

These themes, symbolizing the affective, cognitive, and cultural flavor of the Black psychological perspective, will be discussed in this chapter.

VITALITY

There is a sense of aliveness, animation, emotional vitality, and openness to feelings expressed in the language, oral literature, song, dance (sometimes called the poetry of motion), body language, folk poetry, and expressive thought of Black folks (Redmond, 1971). Black dance and oral literature are described by Jeffers (1971) as being vivacious, exuberant, sensuous, and wholesomely uninhibited, a statement that life should abound and flourish with the vigorous intensity of the Funky Chicken (a dance made popular in the 1960s) rather than the sedateness of the waltz or fox trot. In the Black oral tradition the act of speaking is a performance on the stage of life (Holt, 1975). To capture and hold the attention of the listener, the speaker is expected to make words come alive, to use ear-filling phrases that stir the imagination with heavy reliance on tonal rhymes, symbolism, figures of speech, and personification. The vitality expressed in Black language is life-affirming; despair, apathy, and downtroddenness are rejected. Feelings are not suppressed, but freely shared with others. The speaker, performer, preacher, or singer touches the collective experience base of the listeners by being honest and authentic, telling about life as it really is.

REALNESS—TELLIN' IT LIKE IT IS

The message expressed in the folk poetry of the blues and gospel music is that profound sorrow, pain, hardship, and struggle cannot be avoided. The blues singer opens up the window of his or her soul and tells it like it 'tis. Life does not play with Black folks. Disappointment, tragedy, setbacks, and defeat are inevitable. There are dues to be paid, nobody gets away clean. This is simply the way things are (Neal, 1972). The first step of learning to survive is to see life exactly as it is, without self-deception or romantic pieties. The story of the blues and gospel lyrics is not, however, one of resignation or despair. In the Black ethos, tragedy, defeat and disappointment are not equated with psychological destruction. The goal of a Black presence in the face of tragedy is to keep on keepin' on, to keep the faith, to maintain a cool steadiness, and to keep on climbin' until one has transcended. Langston Hughes (1954) conveys the steadiness, persistence, and toughness of Black folks in the face of hardship in his poem, "Mother to Son," where an aging Black mother is breaking down the facts of life she has learned through experience to her young son. She sums it up by telling him:

> Life for me ain't been no crystal stair.
> It's had tacks in it,
> And splinters,
> And boards torn up,
> And places with no carpet on the floor—
> Bare.
> But all the time
> I'se been a-climbin' on
> And reachin' landin's,
> And turnin' corners
> And sometimes going' in the dark
> Where there ain't been no light.
> So boy, don't you turn your back.
> Don't you set down on the steps
> 'Cause you finds it kinder hard.
> Don't you fall now—
> For I'se still going', honey,
> I'se still climbin'
> And life for me ain't been no crystal stair."[1]

Gladys Knight (1973), a modern-day rhythm and blues singer, describes the Black presence in the face of tragedy as being a situation where "I've got to use my imagination to make the best of a bad situation to keep on keepin' on."[2]

Psychological growth and emotional maturity cannot be completed until the person has paid his or her dues by overcoming hardship, defeat, sorrow, and grief (Baldwin, 1963). The person who has come through the storm is no longer afraid and his or her soul may look back and wonder how they made it over the troubled sea of life. He or she has a healthy respect for life, is not afraid to be real, authentic, or genuine, is aware of his or her own vulnerability and has the capacity to be compassionate and emphatic with the struggles of others.

RESILIENCE AND REVITALIZATION

The picture of human existence presented by the "Blues People" (Jones, 1963) and the gospel artists goes beyond oppression, hardship, and struggle. There is more to life than unrequited love, two-timing women, unbearable sorrow, and run-down neighborhoods. On the other side of the ledger to balance the emotional and psychological spectrum are the renewal experiences of sensuousness, joy, and laughter. The trouble will pass, the blues won't last always, and freedom will emerge on some bright sunshiny day.

The consciousness of pain, sorrow, and hurt in blues and gospel music is not accompanied by feelings of guilt, shame, and self-rejection. It is a pure sadness that can be differentiated from the clinical syndrome of depression where guilt, shame, and self-debasement make it easier to draw upon the revitalization powers of sensuousness, joy, and laughter. The blues singer, despite the pain of loss, grief, and defeat, is fully aware of the excitement and euphoria of sensuality; he or she knows that, "A good looking woman will make a bull dog gnaw his bone." Reference to the pleasures of sexuality is explicit in the blues with lyrics like, "My baby rocks me with one steady roll."[3] If terminal illness prevents one from looking forward to future renewal experiences through sensuality, then one can look back with the satisfaction that, "I have had my fun if I don't get well no more."

Church-going Black folks are open to being moved by the spirit to peak experiences of joy, happiness, and euphoria. Those who erroneously label gospel music as sorrow songs miss the transcendent theme of dark clouds passing, the hopefulness of being bound for higher ground, and the joy of being touched by the spirit. The ability to stay in touch with the energizing process generated by the uplifting experiences of feeling good, sensuality, and joy had enabled Black folks to revitalize, keep the faith, keep on keepin' on, and keep on climbin'.

The themes of sensuality and joy in the oral literature of Black folks are complemented by the presence of laughter. Blacks use humor as a weapon to confront adversity (Davis, 1968; Lomax, 1961). One of the primary topics of Black humor historically was the absurdity of racial oppression in a Christian nation. Levine (1977) describes a comical anecdote emphasizing how restrictive Southern racial codes forced Black folks to invert their natural inclinations. A Black man accidentally falls from a tall building, suddenly in midair he realizes that he is going to land on a White woman. The brother forces himself to reverse direction in midair and lands back on top of the building. Black humor expressed by social critics like Godfrey Cambridge (1961) and Richard Pryor (1975) goes right to the heart of troublesome social-political realities while avoiding the inane, slapstick frivolousness of the Bud Abbott-Lou Costello variety. Tragedy and comedy are juxtaposed so that the same situation simultaneously invokes laughter and tears.

The prototype of realism in Black comedy is Jesse B. Simple, a fictional underemployed urban Black male living in Harlem in the 1940s and 1950s created by Langston Hughes (1950, 1953, and 1957), better known as Simple. Through Jess Simple, Hughes used a sardonic, poignant, gallows-type humor to discuss life in Black America. Simple worked for white folks in a low-status job downtown during the week. His social commentary on economic conditions, male-female relationships, racial oppression, growing up in the South, Black pride, struggling for survival, and the resiliency of Black folks takes place in Patty's Bar, Simple's favorite after-work hangout. The flavor of Simple's penetrating wit can be captured from the passage below, where Simple, who is recovering from a bout of pneumonia, identifies all the tragedies that can happen to a Black man as he passes through the world. The second person in Simple's narration is an anonymous straight man:

> "Not only am I half dead right now from pneumonia, but everything else has happened to me! I have been cut, shot, stabbed, run over, hit by a car, and tromped by a horse. I have been robbed, fooled, deceived, two-timed, double-crossed, dealt seconds, and might near black-mailed—but I am still here."

> "You're a tough man," I said.

> "I have been fired, laid off, and last week given an indefinite vacation, also Jim Crowed, segregated, barred out, insulted, eliminated, called black, yellow, and red, locked in, locked out, locked up, and also left holding the bag. I have been caught in the rain, caught in the raids, caught short with my rent, and caught with another man's wife. In my time I have been caught—but I am still here!"

> "You have suffered," I said.

> "Suffered!" cried Simple. "My mamma should have named me Job instead of Jess Semple. I have been underfed, underpaid, undernourished, and everything but undertaken. I been bit by dogs, cats, mice, rats, poll parrots, fleas, chiggers, bedbugs, granddaddies, mosquitoes, and a gold-toothed woman."

> "Great day in the morning!"

> "That ain't all," said Simple. "In this life I been abused, confused, misused, accused, false-arrested, tried, sentenced, paroled, black-jacketed, beat, third-degreed, and near about lynched."

> "Anyhow, your health has been good—up to now," I said.

> "Good health nothing," objected Simple, waving his hands, kicking off the cover, and swinging his feet out of bed. "I done had everything from flat feet to a flat head. Why, man, I was born with measles! Since then I had smallpox, whooping cough, croup, appendicitis, athlete's foot, tonsillitis, arthritis, backache, mumps, and a strain—but I am still here, Daddy-o, I'm still here!"

> "Having survived all that, what are you afraid of, now that you are almost over pneumonia?"

> "I'm afraid," said Simple, "I will die before my time."[4]

The willingness to laugh in the face of misfortune without denying the seriousness of adverse reality is part of the survival equipment of Afro-Americans. Humor grounded in reality is psychologically refreshing; it defines the situation in manageable terms and prevents the build-up of unbearable anxieties by not allowing people to take themselves too seriously. Soul is the ability to laugh while growing with hardships, paying dues, and transcending tragedies.

The power of the words of blues singers, folk poets, comedians, and preachers to uplift, heal, inspire, and revitalize comes in large measure from their adeptness in reaching out to touch others with messages from a shared pool of experiences that both speaker and listener can bear witness to. In the act of touching others through a shared experienced frame, the individuals know that they are not alone, that they are psychologically connected to others who can affirm the actuality of their experiences. In the Black church the preacher physically touches the parishioner with the "laying of the hands" in the presence of others to symbolize that the person being touched has not been spiritually forsaken or abandoned. In *The Fire Next Time*, Baldwin describes the psychological impact of sharing, witnessing, closeness, embracing, and affirmation from his days as a teenage preacher in a Harlem storefront church. During an adolescent identity crisis Baldwin fell to the floor of the church in a fit of guilt-induced panic. While he was on the floor all night, the church members rejoiced and prayed "over me to bring me through, and in the morning they raised me and told me I was saved." Baldwin goes on to describe the drama and excitement he felt when the church came together in one harmonious voice:

> There is no music like that music, no drama like the drama of saints rejoicing, the sinners moaning, the tambourines racing, and all those voices coming together and crying holy unto the Lord. There is still, for me, no pathos quite like the pathos of those multicolored, worn, somehow triumphant and transfigured faces, speaking from the

depths of a visible, tangible, continuing despair of the goodness of the Lord. I have never seen anything to equal the fire and excitement that sometimes, without warning, fill a church, causing the church, as Leadbelly and so many others have testified, to "rock." Nothing that has happened to me since equals the power and the glory that I sometimes felt when, in the middle of a sermon, I knew I was somehow, by some miracle really carrying, as they said, "the Word"— when the Church and I were one. Their pain and their joy were mine, and mine were theirs—they surrendered their pain and joy to me, I surrendered mine to them—and their cries of "Amen!" and "Hallelujah!" and "Yes, Lord," and "Praise His Name!" and "Preach It, brother!" sustained and whipped on my solos until we all became equal, wringing wet, singing and dancing, in anguish and rejoicing, at the foot of the altar."[5]

INTERDEPENDENCE, INTERRELATEDNESS, CONNECTEDNESS, AND SYNTHESIS

In the theoretical model of Black psychology presented by Wade Nobles (1976), interrelatedness, connectedness, and interdependence are viewed as the unifying philosophic concepts in the Afro-American experience base. The concepts are prominent themes in Black language with respect to the interactive dynamics between speaker and listener, the power of words to control, cognitive style, timing, and communicative competence. The spoken word in the Black community is the pervasive force that connects human experiences. Human contact, the connecting linkage between people, is established by the spoken word. Through the spoken word linkages are established across time and space, transmitting the Afro-American heritage from one generation to another.

The language of soul folks—whether it occurs on street corners, in beauty shops, barber shops, parties, love raps, playgrounds, or in political speeches and church sermons—is characterized by the interrelatedness of speaker and listener.

The act of speaking is a dramatic presentation of one's person-
hood to those who share a background of similar acculturation
(Holt, 1975). The listener acts as an echo chamber, repeating,
cosigning, validating, and affirming the message of the
speaker with amens, right-ons, yes sirs, teach-ons, and you
aint' never lieds. The speaker sends out a call and the listener
responds. During this call-response dialogue, the speaker and
listener are joined together in a common psycholinguistic
space. Each participant has the opportunity to expand the
message through amplification and repetition. Spillers (1971)
illustrates the interactive interchange between speaker and
listener by recalling a sermon and the accompanying amen
corner from her childhood that went something like this:

PREACHER: The same Christ, the same man.
CONGREGATION: Same man.
PREACHER: Who sits high and looks low, who rounded the world
in the middle of his hands?
CONGREGATION: Middle of his hands.
PREACHER: The same man who fed 5,000 and still had some left
over.
CONGREGATION: Yes sir! Had some left.
PREACHER: The same man who raised the dead and who walked
the waters and calmed the seas.
CONGREGATION: Let's hold him up church.
PREACHER: This same man is looking out for you and me.[6]

The Black speaker establishes a form of situational control
vis-á-vis the listener by defining a reality using vivid imagery
drawn from a body of collective experiences that others understand and can relate to events in their life space (Holt,
1975). The speaker controls the situation linguistically with
words that touch the psychoaffective rhythms, activating
emotions of joy, laughter, sadness, strength, optimism, and
feelings that power and control over Black destiny by Black
people in a racist society can become a reality. Describing the
collective experience of oppression with tonal rhymes like "we
have been abused, misused, refused, and confused," Black

speakers draw a picture of reality that their listeners can cosign and affirm. Martin Luther King, Jr. used metaphors to describe the reality that Black people were not satisfied with the slow pace of the civil rights legislation in August of 1963 and we would not be satisfied until, "Justice rolls down like water and righteousness like a mighty stream."[7] When Stokeley Carmichael used the term "Black power," Black folks intuitively knew that he meant Black folks must control the reality of what was going down in their community. Later, he wrote a book on Black power (1967) to explain what he meant so that White folks could understand.

The extensive use of metaphor in Black speech reflects a cognitive style where likeness, correspondence, similarity, and analogous relationships between ideas, events, and concepts are shown by using picturesque imagery that appeals conjointly to the intellect and emotions. Inner-city youth speak of successful sexual encounters as "hitting the jill pot" (Holt, 1975). King (1963) paints a picture comparing the exhausting struggle against the evil consequences of oppression as having left people "battered by the storms of persecution and staggered by the winds of police brutality."[8] The metaphor in this case creates an analogous relationship between evils of Jim Crow justice and being "battered by the storms and staggered by the winds."

In Black speech the words come alive through colorful poetic sketches that arouse feelings. The speaker uses visual symbols to draw a picture of what's happening. The intellectual meaning is carried by implication creating a psychoaffective or cognitive-affective synthesis (Smitherman, 1977). Holt captures the cognitive-affective syntheses in the visual imagery expressed by Black youth in the following statements:

- gettin over like a fat rat in a cheese factory
- that aint nothing man, ice it
- higher than nine kites on a breezy day

- man that dude was really stroking
- just as cool as she wanted to be
- I don't know what page you on
- you on the wrong channel, tune it
- Jim he was faking it and making it
- I'm gonna put your hip boots on
- Lay out till you get wired up
- Layin on the cut till I'm hipped
- Freeze that shit and space[9]

The metaphor in Black language is a teaching device (Spillers, 1971). Speakers depend on the common background between themselves and their listeners to establish impact and associate meanings to the words. Presentation symbols in the form of visual imagery are substituted for abstract concepts to expand and clarify meanings from an Afro-American cultural perspective. Picturesque imagery stimulates the power of the mind to see, to visualize abstract relationships, and to project novel interpretations (Holt, 1975).

Black metaphoric expressions generate multiple meanings. The cultural connotation is conveyed by translating the expression of a figure of speech through an ethnotropic filter delineated by an Afro-American world view. The specific meaning of a statement in a given situation is dependent on contextual cues, coupled with the cultural sophistication and innovativeness of the participants. "Going to meet the man," a folk expression widely used in the Black community, with "the man" symbolizing a White male in authority (who generally ain't givin' the brothers and sisters no slack) can be interpreted to mean going downtown to work in a menial job, going to court to deal with a recalcitrant judge, going to the finance company to explain why the car payment is late, plus a host of other interpretations contingent on the situation. *Going to Meet the Man* is the title of a book of essays by James

Baldwin (1965). In one of the essays, the dying era of blatant Southern racism is symbolized by "the man," a White Southern sheriff who allows the armor of his racism to be slowly penetrated by the vitality, resilience, persistence, courage, humanism, and ultimate righteousness of his adversary, a young Black civil rights worker.

Black children learn to use a linguistic style that is saturated with Black folk expressions, ethnotropisms,[10] metaphors, visual imagery, and figures of speech. They cannot easily translate the isolated words and literal meanings of the conventional Euro-American language they study in school into their normal speech patterns, and their teachers will not permit them to use their normal expressive patterns in the classroom. In his autobiography, *Die Nigger Die*, Rap Brown (1969) describes the conflict arising from his verbal competence in Black expressive styles and the expectation of his teachers with respect to learning traditional English poetry. Running it down to another brother, Rap displays his verbal wizardry by telling him:

> Man you must not know who I am.
> I am sweet peeter jeeter, the womb beater.
> The baby maker the cradle shaker.
> The deer slayer the buck binder the woman finder.
> Known from the gold coast to the rocky shores of Maine.
> Rap is my name and love is my game.[11]

Rap goes on to say "and the teacher expected me to set up in class and study poetry after I could run down stuff like that, if anybody needed to study poetry, she needed to study mine."

The interactive balance between the linguistic rhythms of the speaker and listener characterized by the call-response is synchronized by a reciprocal command of timing and pace. The goal is to be in time with the beat, pulse, tempo, and rhythm of the speech flow. In Martin Luther King's Montgomery speech "We're on the Move," shown in the Montgomery-to-Memphis documentary, an unidentified man stood at King's side repeating the key words, "Yes, suh, we're on the move." The audience picked up the tempo of King's rhythms and reinforced the basic message with the call-response formula:

KING: We can't be dissuaded now.
AUDIENCE: We're on the move.
KING: No wave of racism can stop us now.
AUDIENCE: We're on the move.
KING: Not even the marching of mighty armies can stop us now.
AUDIENCE: We're on the move.

The speaker knows what images, tonal rhythms, metaphors, and stress phrases will generate the interactive sequence because he or she has seen the technique work for others many times (Spillers, 1971). Black adolescents perfect the timing, pace, and rhythm of their language game in peer group interaction by continuously alternating the roles of speaker and listener in verbal interchanges that require active participation, such as playing the Dozens, signifyin', love rappin', lug droppin', and soundin'.

In the Afro-American world view, concepts of timing, rhythm, pace, and sequence extend beyond the dynamics of language to encompass life, history, and the flow of movement in the universe. Human existence, as outlined by King (Lewis, 1971), has a certain repetitive sequence delineated by cycles of oppression, resistance, transcendence, and freedom. Time is eternal and freedom for Black folks is just a matter of time. The rule of Yacob, symbolized in Muslim mythology by the mad scientist who created the evil White person, cannot last forever (Malcolm X, 1965). Both a person and a people must know when to make their move, when to hold on, when to cool it, and when to woof. King perceived the time frame of the civil rights movement, triggered in 1955 by the refusal of Rosa Parks to move to the segregated section of a Birmingham, Alabama bus, as fitting into an historical *Zeitgeist* of resistance that would be followed by an era of freedom and equality. Eldridge Cleaver (1968) viewed Mrs. Parks's historic act and the freedom struggle it initiated as symbolic of a gear shifting somewhere in the universe.

The importance of the spoken word in the Black community is demonstrated by the large number of linguistic terms used to designate different forms of social-linguistic interaction. A list of fifty-four social-linguistic terms compiled by Smith (1974) appears in Table 4.1.

Mastery in the art of skillfully utilizing these social-linguistic categories gives the person access to a wide range of interpersonal interactions, information, and learning situations. The person with a high level of receptive and expressive communicative competence knows how to break it down, how to stay on top of a situation verbally, how to tune in to what others are running down, and, when it is appropriate, how to employ a particular social-linguistic category. The oral tradition is an integral part of Black identity. The emotional, psychological, and cultural tone of the Black ethos is expressed by means of the spoken word. Competence in understanding and interpreting the Black world view, as it is communicated by Black oral expressive styles, comes about as a result of experiences in living and relating to others.

THE VALUE OF DIRECT EXPERIENCE

There is no substitute in the Black ethos for the actual experiences gained in the course of living. The natural facts, eternal truths, wisdom of the ages, and basic precepts of survival emerge from the experiences of life: "you cannot lie to life." In

TABLE 4.1.   Terms Used to Designate Social-Linguistic Interaction.

1. Bad Mouth, Mouthin'	28. Mau Mau, Mauing
2. Base, Basin'	29. Mumblin'
3. Blow, Blow on	30. Pimp Talk
4. Call and Response	31. Protection Talk
5. Cappin'	32. Pull Coat
6. Cop a Plea	33. Rappin'
7. Cop on	34. Rhapsodize
8. Cover snatch, Snatchin'	35. Runnin' It Down
9. Dozens, Dirty Dozens	36. Scat Singin'
10. Drop a Dime	37. Screamin'
11. Fat Lip	38. Showboatin'
12. Fat Mouth, Mouthin'	39. Shuckin' and Jivin'
13. Frontin' Off	40. Signify, Signifyin'
14. Gate Mouth, Mouthin	41. Soundin'
15. Gibb, Gibbin' (Jibb)	42. Splib Wibbin'
16. Gripp, Grippin'	43. Stuff Playin'
17. Group, Grouped	44. Sweet Mouthin'
18. High Siding	45. Talkin' Proper
19. Horrah, Horrahin'	46. Talkin' Shit (Talking Trash)
20. Jaw Jackin'	47. Talkin' in Tongue
21. Jeffin'	48. Tautin'
22. Jivin'	49. Testify-Testifyin'
23. Jonin'	50. Toast, Toastin'
24. Larcen, Larcenin'	51. Tom Tom, Tommin'
25. Lolly Gaggin'	52. Whop, Whoppin' Game
26. Lug Droppin'	53. Woffin', Wolfing
27. Mack, Mackin'	54. Woof (Wolf) Ticket

Source: Adapted from E. Smith "Evolution and Continuing Presence of the Oral Tradition in Black America," unpublished doctoral dissertation, University of California-Irvine, 1974. Reprinted by permission.

interpersonal relationships, matters of race, and the affairs of nations, "the truth will out"—no lie can last for long. The truth can stand the test of time and experience; a lie cannot. The slaves kept the faith in the belief that freedom was just a matter of time (how long? not long), the experience of captivity would pass because slavery was against the laws of God and humanity.

A person who lacks in mother wit, the common sense of life experiences, and who flaunts untested book knowledge is perceived in the Black idiom as an educated fool. Sometimes college brothers and sisters, after a few courses in economic theory and sociology, come home in the summer and expound the theoretical principles of Marxism, Keynesian economics, stagflation, and supply-side economic theory to the community folks. They are usually stopped short by such questions as, "When do it get me a job?" *The Best and the Brightest* of David Halberstam (1971) refused to heed the lessons of the unsuccessful experiences of the French in Vietnam. They went ahead with their elaborate geopolitical theories, computer-based technologies, and body count projections only to get themselves deeper and deeper into a no-win situation. The brothers on the corner, without the benefit of computer-based technology and elaborate geopolitical theory, said from the gate, "You ain't got no business puttin' your foot on another man's land." Time and experience proved them right.

The collective lessons of experience are carried forward from one generation to the next by the oral tradition. Children are taught the precepts of life through a vast oral literature consisting of parables, folk verses, folk tales, biblical verses, songs, and proverbs. Many older Black adults can remember hearing these sayings from their parents and grandparents.

- The truth will out.
- Don't sign no checks with your mouth that your ass can't cash.
- Hard head make a soft behind.
- You better be yourself or you gonna be by yourself.
- One monkey don't stop no show.
- Only a fool plays the golden rule in a crowd that don't play fair.
- If you lay down with dogs you gonna come up with fleas.
- What goes around, comes around.

- You better learn how to work before work works you.
- You don't git to be old being no fool.

Each generation has to refashion and expand the meaning of the proverbial wisdom to encompass the events of their time and place. In a moment of deep contemplation during a Harlem racial riot a few hours after his father's funeral, James Baldwin (1955) found himself reflecting on the meaning of life contained in his father's parables, sermons, and verses. Like many adolescents and young adults, he had come to the conclusion that the values represented in the collective experience of his father's dictums were meaningless. Now, in the hour of his father's death, amidst the destruction going on around him, Baldwin saw the familiar texts and songs arranged before him like empty bottles "waiting to hold the meaning which life would give them for me."[12] Since that time Baldwin has filled the empty bottles with his own experiences combined with a more mature understanding of the collective ethos transmitted by his father. Utilizing his "gift of tongues" (Warren, 1965), Baldwin has gone on to articulate and enlarge on the Black world view. In a series of articles, plays, essays, and novels, Baldwin has carried the word forth to the next generation. This is his legacy. Nothing is ever escaped. Dues must be paid, and tragedy is necessary for personal growth. The revitalization of the human spirit comes about through love, sensuousness, joy, and laughter.

The notion of psychological growth arising from discoveries initiated by life experiences is evident in the autobiographies of Richard Wright (1945, 1977) and Malcolm X (1965). Richard Wright started out believing in the Protestant ethic of hard work, self-control, personal initiative, resourcefulness, and future planning, only to discover the pervasiveness of structural racism in America, both North and South. His determination to write about life in Black America exactly as he experienced it, with racism as a more prevailing force than economic class, provided him with the motivation to keep on climbin' and ultimately caused the demise of his flirtation with the Communist party.

Malcolm X goes through several transitions as he progresses experientially from a child in a nearly all-White farming community of the Midwest to his ultimate break with the Lost Found Nation of Islam. After being discouraged from considering a career in law by his White elementary school teacher, Malcolm X moved on to brief tenures in the Negro jobs of that day in Boston and New York; shoeshine boy, coach boy on the railroads, and waiter. Subsequently, as a young adult he drifted into street hustling, petty crime, and burglary, which landed him in prison. In prison he embraced the faith of the Black Muslim Nation of Islam, and after his release became an activist under the tutelage of his father figure, mentor, and role model Elijah Muhammad. During his experience as an activist minister he discovered that the narrow religious band of nationalism espoused by the Nation of Islam was too confining to produce the changes in America necessary to bring about a wider range of choices for Black folks. He became convinced by the dictates of his own experience that, in order to consolidate his identity and generate a broader platform of social change, it would be necessary for him to seek his independence from the Nation of Islam.

The relationship between identity and life experiences comes together in Ralph Ellison's *Invisible Man* (1952). The invisible man, the protagonist without a name to symbolize the invisible presence of Black people in the mainstream of American life, goes through a series of transformations before he discovers that attempts to avoid coming to grips with the struggle to define who he really is by becoming a carbon copy of someone else are doomed to fail. As a college student and later as a social activist, with the in-between time spent as an angry rebel, the protagonist tries to become a facsimile of his mentors, only to feel disillusioned and betrayed when he finds out that his role models are not what they appear to be. Sitting alone in a cellar at the end of the novel, he gradually comes to the unavoidable conclusion that nothing is ever escaped. He painfully discovers that, in order to achieve his identity, he can no longer become a duplicate of someone else; he must confront his existence and take the responsibility for sorting things out by listening to the internal voice of his experience.

Older people in the Black community are the reservoirs of the wisdom accumulated during the experiences of a lifetime. They are the storehouses of the oral tradition and the keepers of the heritage. The elderly are valued because they have been through the experiences that can only come with age. They have been "down the line" as the saying goes, seen the comings and goings of life, and been through the repetitive cycles of oppression, struggle, survival, backlash, and renewed struggle. Older people have stood the test of time and adversity, paid their dues, transcended tragedy, and learned how to keep on keepin' on. According to Richard Pryor, "You learn something when you listen to old people, they ain't all fools cause you don't git to be old bein' no fool, lotta young wise men deader than a mother...![13] The presence of older people provides a seasoned steadiness during troubled times in the Black extended family. Bill Withers (1971), in the song called "Grandma's Hands," sings about the soothing impact Black grandmothers have on troubled young adults and the comforting effect of their affection on children.

In the *Children of Ham*, Claude Brown (1973) presents a quasi-fictitious group of Harlem teenagers who have banded together in an extended family. They live in abandoned tenement buildings and survive the dangers of the streets by mutual support, mother wit, and resourcefulness. One of the young women, Dee Dee, takes up fortune telling, a money-making business in Harlem. Women get together in homes and beauty parlors on Saturday nights for tea leaf and palm reading parties fortified with pots of pig's feet, neck bones, and collard greens. Dee Dee has checked out the whole gamut of tea leaf reading, roots, horoscopes, astrology, tarot cards, clairvoyance, and soothsaying. She found out, however, that the clientele won't trust her with their innermost secrets because she is too young to have been around long enough to know what life is all about. Dee Dee, who is also into drama, is trying to figure out how to convey the appearance of age by acting the part of an older woman. She thinks that, if she can create the impression of being an older woman, her customers will feel confident that she has the requisite experiences to render sound advice. Dee Dee considers getting a way-out name like Madam Zooloo or Sister Buzzard, wearing a wig, changing her manner of dress, learning to walk differently, slowing down the movements of her hands, not turning too fast, and decreasing the level of her pep and energy, because when people get old they naturally slow down.

There are periodic reports that the White elderly feel abandoned, useless, alone, and terrified by the prospect of death (Clark and Gosnell, 1977). Old Black folks, on the other hand, are an integral part of the community. They are resilient, and they know how to survive, get over, get down, socialize, and do the old folks romance with members of the opposite sex. The Black elderly have completed the seasons of life, experienced the ongoing sequence of birth and death, kept the faith, and are no longer terrified by the eventuality of their own death.

Death in the Black community is perceived as a celebration of life, a testament to the fact that a life has been lived, that the earthly journey has been completed. Those who serve as witnesses in the presence of death—extended family, friends, and church members—to affirm the essence of the person's existence are ready to testify to the fact that the deceased has fought the battle, borne the burden, and finished the course; they are ready to understand and say, "Well done." Unlike the Euro-American culture, where death is suppressed and the dead and dying are isolated from public view (Aries, 1980), the passing of life in the Black ethos is an occasion where public festivities are part of the mourning process. In the Black community of New Orleans, the funeral is commemorated with a parade to the cemetery, complete with a jazz band to start the deceased on the next leg of the journey. After the funeral, mourners get together to eat, drink, and talk about happy times with the deceased. The upbeat tone of death in the Black experience has been noted by informal observers. Shortly after the assassination of Robert Kennedy in June of 1968, his sister-in-law, Jacqueline Kennedy Onassis, was talking to Frank Mankiewicz, Kennedy's campaign manager about how the Catholic church was at its best at the time of death. She went on to say, "I'll tell you who else understands death are the Black churches. I remember at the funeral of Martin Luther King. I was looking at those faces, and I realized they know death. They see it all the time and they're ready for it."[14]

DISTRUST AND DECEPTION

The experiences of slavery, Jim Crow legislation, de facto and de jure segregation, institutional racism, and the on-going economic oppression in America have taught Black folks to distrust White folk. Too many dreams have been deferred and promissory notes unpaid by the banks of justice for Blacks to be able to trust the White person's word, laws, and institutions. Above all, the destiny of Afro-Americans cannot be placed in the hands of the Whites. The trust-mistrust issue was at the heart of the great debate during the post-reconstruction period at the turn of the twentieth century between the accommodationist, Booker T. Washington, and the militant-activist, W. E. B. DuBois. DuBois (1903) was of the opinion that Black folks should not passively surrender their civil, legal, and political rights, guaranteed under the equal protection clause of the Fourteenth Amendment, and depend on the good will of White folks to return these rights when they felt Blacks had demonstrated that they were ready to assume the responsibilities of full citizenship.

The distrust of White folks was a favorite topic at street corner rallies conducted by the Harlem race of men of a bygone era, Garveyites, curbstone nationalists of all kinds, and members of the Nation of Islam. Drawing on the collective experience of their audiences with White folks, speakers had no trouble producing an uncontested response when they asked rhetorical questions about who was the biggest liar, thief, hypocrite, or gangster in the world. Elijah Muhammad, leader of the Lost Found Nation of Islam in the Wilderness of the North American continent, told it like it was and still is when he accused Whites of engaging in a posture of "trickno-logy" in their relationships with Black folks (Baldwin, 1963). Stokely Carmichael (1971) repeatedly drew spontaneous affir-mation from Black gatherings around the country when he called the White person a liar, hypocrite, and thief, who stole this country from the Indians, lock, stock and barrel, top to bottom, left to right. The Native Americans themselves cos-igned Stokely's statement about the theft of the country. In *Bury My Heart at Wounded Knee* (D. Brown, 1970), an aging Indian chief, talks about the broken promises: "The White man made us many promises, more than I can remember, but they never kept but one; they promised to take our land and they took."[15] When President Lyndon Johnson was accused by the news media of a credibility gap in communicating his policies on the Vietnam War, Stokely came right down in front with his response when he said, "Credibility gap, hell, that honkey is just lying." The Kerner commission (1968), created by the Johnson administration to study the causes of urban unrest, rebellions, and violence in America's Black ghettos, after doc-umenting the history of White racism in America, concluded that Black folks had valid reasons to distrust White institutions, promises, and illusions of significant progress in the elimination of racial oppression.

The Black revolutionaries of the late 1960s, The so-called "Angry Children of Malcolm X" (Lester, 1971), went a step further with the issue of distrust, raising doubts about the substance of Euro-American values. They saw the White culture as decadent, lacking in humanistic concern for others, and predicted the ultimate death of White civilization with the emergence of a new order of human values based on respect for human dignity. These young activists left us with the question, "Who would want to integrate with a burning house?"

Distrust of the White man, his word, his technology, and his woman is the message expressed in the epic poem "Shine." Shine is the only Black person aboard the supposedly unsinkable Titanic, "the biggest and baddest ship to ever sail the seas"[16] (Simpkins et al., 1977), when it starts on its ill-fated maiden voyage across the Atlantic. Amidst the luxury and splendor of this vast ocean liner, Shine is employed as a laborer in the boiler room, shoveling coal to keep the furnace going. After the ship hits the iceberg and water begins to flood the boiler room, Shine becomes concerned about what's happening and starts to go up on deck to check for himself. The boiler room chief, who has faith in the ship's technology, tells Shine:[17]

> Shine, Shine, get back below.
> I got forty-nine brand new electric pumps to keep that water back.

Shine, who concludes from his direct observation that the ship is sinking, tells the chief:

> That may be true and there is little doubt,
> But I'll be goddamned if I'll stay here and find out.
> I don't like chicken and I don't like ham,
> And I don't believe your pumps is worth a damn.

Had he lived in the modern era Shine might have added that "the will of people is greater than man's technology." As the epic continues:

> *When Shine stepped up on the quarter deck,*
> *The symphony orchestra was playing near oh my God to thee;*
> *And the sharks in the water were singing Shine, oh, Shine,*
> *Bring your Black ass to me.*

Shine replies to the shark:

> *I know you outswim the barracuda,*
> *Outsmart every fish in the sea*
> *But you got to be a stroking mother…to outswim me.*

After Shine dives in the water and demonstrates his aquatic skills, the rich White man, aware of impending doom, begs Shine to return and save him with pleas of:

> *Shine, Shine, save poor me,*
> *And I'll make you rich as any Shine can be.*

Shine, no doubt recalling the history of broken promises, tells the man:

> *There is money on land and money on sea*
> *But the money on land is better for me.*
> *One thing about you white folks I couldn't understand*
> *You all wouldn't offer me that money when we was all on land.*

The poem ends with:

> *Now, Shine could swim and Shine could float,*
> *Could hit more licks than a motor boat,*
> *Shine swam the Atlantic and swam the Pacific,*
> *When the Titanic finally sunk*
> *Shine was walkin' round in Alabama, dead drunk.*

In view of the distrust Afro-Americans have developed in their dealings with White folks, it should come as no surprise that Black folks have been less than honest, even somewhat deceptive, when it comes to sharing what's really on their minds with White folks, as can be seen in the following statements taken from old slave songs and narratives:

> Got one mind for white folk to see
> Nother for what I know is me
> He don't know don't know what's on my mind.[18]

> You t'inks I'm mistaken, honey! But I know t'ings dat de wite folks wid all dar larnin' nebber fin's out, an' nebber sarches fo' nudder...

> No, honey! De good lawd doan gib ebery-ting to his wite chilluns. He's gib' em de wite skin an' larnin'. An' he's made 'em rich and free. But de brack folks is his chilluns, too, an' he gibs us de brack skin an' no larnin', an' hab makes us to' work fo' de wite folks. But de good Lawd gib us eyes t' see t'ings dey doan see, an' tells me be patient, 'cause dar's no wite nor brack in hebben. An' de time's commin' when he'll make his brack chilluns free in dis yere worl', an gib' em larnin', and' good homes, an' good times. Ah! honey, I knows, I knows![19]

> Aunt Aggy—a Virginia slave in the 1840s

The use of a common language with culturally different semantics enables Blacks to conceal what they mean from White folks while still maintaining a high level of clarity in their communications. Words, phrases, and statements that are taken to mean one thing when interpreted from a Euro-American frame of reference can mean something entirely different when translated through an Afro-American ethnotropic filter. Familiar gospel tunes sung right under old mass's nose, like "Steal Away to Jesus," "On My Journey Now," and "Dis Train is Bound For Glory," depending on the nature of subtle contextual cues, could be interpreted to mean, "I'm getting ready to steal away from here, to start on my journey on a secret train [the underground railroad] bound north to freedom." The implicit determination to stride toward freedom hidden in the multiple meanings of Black gospel music was quickly captured by the nonviolent warriors of the civil rights movement as they adjusted the beat of their marching orders to songs like "Got on My Travelin' Shoes," "We Shall Not Be Moved," "Ain't Gonna Let Nobody Turn Me 'Round," and "Woke Up This Morning with My Mind Set on Freedom."

Linguistic deception can be used as a way of controlling undesirable psychological imagery and devaluative labels propogated by Euro-Americans. A bad nigger in the White folklore is someone who is undesirable. In the cultural semantics of Black folks a bad nigger is a hero, someone who is looked up to for not being afraid to take the risk of standing up to White folks. Black children sometimes confuse their teachers by turning undesirable labels around to indicate admirable personality traits. Teachers apply terms like "clumsy lips," suggesting speech deficits, to children who persistently use Black English in the classroom. When the children refer to somebody as having clumsy lips, they mean a brother who can "run it down, talk that talk, and get over" with the power of words (Holt, 1975).

Black teenagers are able to control the flow of conversation in interviews with White authority figures when they shift cultural referents to Black figures of speech and start talking about "holding down corners," "breaking down," "doing the penguin," "messin' with pigs," and "shooting" at fine "foxes."[20] White teenagers trying to copy the language of Black teenagers often get the semantics mixed up; witness the situation where a White girl refers to a big ugly White boy as a "fox."

A classic case of Blacks controlling powerful White folks by a psychology of deception based on the counter tricknology of linguistic nuances, seeming agreement, and some gold old-fashioned Sambo-like shuffling, grinnin', and tommin' is Dr. Bledsoe in Ellison's (1952) *Invisible Man*. In a long, rambling tirade excerpted below, Dr. Bledsoe, the president of a small Black Southern college, explains the realities of power, control, counter tricknology, and deception in Black-White relationships to an errant protege. The student protege, the unnamed protagonist of Ellison's novel, has endangered the college's existence by exposing a White benefactor to an incestuous Black family and also to a group of mentally deranged but politically astute Black professional lawyers and doctors who were supposed to remain hidden away from the prying eyes of White folks. When the student defends his behavior by explaining that he stopped at these locations because the benefactor "ordered me to," Dr. Bledsoe takes off on him:

> "Ordered you?" he said. "He ordered you. Dammit, white folks are always giving orders, it's a habit with them. Why didn't you make an excuse? Couldn't you say they had sickness—smallpox—or picked another cabin? Why that Trueblood shack? My God, boy! You're Black and living in the South—did you forget how to lie?"

> "But I was only trying to please him..."

> "Please him? And here you are a junior in college! Why, the dumbest black bastard in the cotton patch knows that the only way to please a white man is to tell him a lie! What kind of education are you getting around here?"

After the protagonist threatens to report him to the trustees, Dr. Bledsoe continues:

> "Boy, you are a fool," he said. "Your white folks didn't teach you anything and your mother-wit has left you cold. What has happened to you young Negroes? I thought you had caught on to how things are done down here. Boy you don't even know the difference between the way things are and the way they're supposed to be. My God," he gasped, "what is the race coming to? Why, boy, you can tell anyone you like—sit down there...Sit down, sir, I say!"

> "Tell anyone you like," he said. "I don't care. I wouldn't raise my little finger to stop you. Because I don't owe anyone a thing, son. Who, Negroes? Negroes don't control this school or much of anything else—haven't you learned even that? No, sir, they don't control this school, nor white folk either. True they support it, but I control it. I's big and black and I say 'Yes, suh' as loudly as any burrhead when it's

convenient, but I'm still the king down here. I don't care how much it appears otherwise. Power doesn't have to show off. Power is confident, self-assuring, self-starting and self-stopping, self-warming and self-justifying. When you have it, you know it. Let the Negroes snicker and the crackers laugh! Those are the facts, son. The only ones I even pretend to please are big white folk, and even those I control more than they control me. This is a power set-up, son, and I'm at the controls. You think about that. When you buck against me, you're bucking against power, rich white folk's power, the nation's power—which means government power!"[21]

SUMMARY

The Black psychological perspective, embodied in the qualities of emotional vitality, realness, resilience, interrelatedness, the value of direct experience, and distrust and deception, determines how events are experienced, interpreted, and expressed in the phenomenal field. The failure to acknowledge the existence of a Black psychological perspective or frame of reference has been a source of controversy between Blacks and Whites in behavioral science research, education, psychotherapy, child development, and family life. Furthermore, communication between Blacks and Whites about complex social realities is problematic because they may not be looking at the issues, such as racial progress, police brutality, and control of the decision-making apparatus, from a common psychological perspective. In order to move toward resolving the conflicts associated with differences in cultural and psychological perspectives between Blacks and Whites, it is essential that the Black perspective be taken into consideration by the policy-making bodies in behavioral science research, social services planning, community mental health, and education.

CHAPTER FIVE

EDUCATIONAL ACHIEVEMENT AMONG AFRICAN-AMERICANS[1]

Any discussion of the educational achievement of African-American youngsters should be preceded by a general summary of the current state of affairs in the field of education, and how Black youngsters are now faring. Perhaps the most appropriate place to begin is with a general overview.

In the first edition of *The Psychology of Blacks*, White (1984) painted a dismal picture of the educational system and the progress, or lack of it, that Black youngsters were making in it. His statement of the problem generally suggested that the longer Black children remain on the educational conveyor belt, the farther behind they fall. A contemporary update of the academic progress and achievement of African-American youngsters reveals little if any change from the dismal reports of the 1960s.

ACADEMIC PROFILE

A series of reports on the American educational system appeared in the early 1980s (National Commission on Excellence in Education, 1983; Goodlad, 1983; Task Force on Education and Economic Growth, 1983), and all commented on the overall failure of the educational system in preparing America's youth. To quote from *A Nation at Risk*, the most heralded report at the time:

> We report to the American people that while we can take justifiable pride in what our schools and colleges have historically accomplished and contributed to the United States and the well being of its people, the educational foundations of our society are presently being eroded by a rising tide of mediocrity that threatens our very future as a nation and a people.

To support this claim, the report cites, among other data, that 23 million adults are functionally illiterate, that there has been a decline over the last seventeen years in SAT scores (a 50-point average decline for verbal scores, a 40-point average decline for mathematics) and that, according to most standardized tests, high school students are achieving at lower rates than they were some twenty-six years ago when Sputnik was launched.

The academic profile of minority youth, particularly African-Americans, is especially disturbing. Among African-Americans, 59.8 percent have completed high school while 11.1 percent have completed four more years of college. African-American youngsters typically lag behind their Anglo mates on almost every objective index of academic achievement. Most reports conclude that, on standardized tests, average achievement scores of African-American youngsters in all subject areas are generally one standard deviation below their Anglo age mates.

In addition, the national assessment of education progress (NEAP) measures achievement of youngsters at ages nine, thirteen, and seventeen, in seven content areas including reading-literature-comprehension, music, art, citizenship, social studies, science, and mathematics. In tests administered from 1975 through 1982, African-American youngsters, in each age category, scored several points below the mean in each of seven content areas.[1]

African-American children seem to start their educational lives with cognitive, sensory, and motor skills equal to their Anglo age mates, yet academic achievement levels for them seem to decrease with the length of time they stay in school. It would not be uncommon to find, for example, that African-American children have fallen form one to three grade levels behind their White peers by the time they are in high school. African-American youngsters also seem three times more likely to be labeled as educable mentally retarded and to be enrolled in remedial educational programs. They are also half as likely to be enrolled in programs for gifted students.

The illiteracy rate for African-Americans (44 percent) is more than two and one-half times that of Whites. Their high school dropout rates also continue to be high. Entrance rates into college for African-Americans also decreased over the last several years. In the late seventies, slightly over 50 percent of African-American high school graduates entered college. By the early eighties, the proportion of African-Americans entering college had dropped to 36 percent. In California, for example, less than 4.5 percent of Black high school graduates are eligible for admission to a University of California school; and less than 11 percent are eligible for admission to one of the nineteen California State University campuses.

It should also be pointed out that many African-American youngsters attend schools "in crisis." Several reports document a growing number of cases of violence (e.g., student-student, student-teacher) and vandalism. Many of these same schools also have fewer experienced teachers, as well as less than adequate teaching equipment and facilities.

To say that the educational attainment profile of African-American youngsters just presented paints a rather dismal and discouraging picture is a gross understatement. The travesty of this situation is all too apparent and the prospects of any positive, substantive change occurring in the very near future appears remote. Yet these are the precise social and educational conditions under which the majority of African-American children live and are educated.

Given the negative profile for African-American educational achievement, many in our society are tempted to conclude that Blacks in general, and Black youth in particular, are simply unmotivated, unable, and/or unwilling to achieve academically. However, despite these distressing statistics, it may be inaccurate to assume that motivation in African-American youngsters is absent and achievement is not taking place. On the contrary, motivation is alive and well and achievement is taking place, but maybe not in ways we are currently measuring or in ways most of us want to talk about.

Certainly, achievement is happening in the arena of athletics where some students pursue sports with a fever of an Olympic competitor. Certainly, achievement is happening in the social arena, where some students pursue social outlets as if their lives would crumble without them. Certainly, achievement is happening in the record industry as more and more Black youths are creating and duplicating new artistic forms (e.g., rap music), which are emulated by Asian youth, Chicano/Latino youth, and White youth. Certainly, achievement is happening interpersonally, where relationships with friends are pursued over relationships with teachers, clergy, public officials, and even parents (all of whom are crucial to the child's intellectual development and progress).

A visual inspection of the Black community might also show that some youths seem more motivated to master the intricacies of selling drugs for profit, or extorting money for protection, than they are motivated to master the intricacies of reading, writing, and counting. But this should be no surprise to us; we could have predicted this phenomenon twenty years ago.

Many well known sociologists and criminologists from the 1960s and 1970s concluded that, if you can indoctrinate a group enough so that they aspire to a particular value system or goal, and you deny them legitimate access to reach that goal, they will develop an illegitimate means to reach that goal. As a matter of fact, this analysis may go a long way to explain the gang violence and illegitimate activity taking place on the streets of our cities all across America. Indeed, these are confusing times that we live in; our youth find themselves no less confusing. In the absence of any social leadership that seeks to correct or eradicate the negative conditions endured by most African-American youth, youth often turn to educators and counselors. However, school systems and classrooms are confusing, unpredictable, and sometimes hostile. There are few, if any, cultural role models, and most Black children will go to school with few opportunities to identify with someone in the classroom that looks like them, especially our young males.

African-Americans are exposed to a curriculum that teaches Hippocrates as the first physician, Pythagoras as the developer of an algebraic formula, and Columbus as the discoverer of America. Yet all of us should know by now that the first physician on the planet was Mhotep, an ancient African-Egyptian, Pythagoras borrowed his algebraic formula from the ancient Egyptians, and Columbus was lost. Is it any wonder that the educational system has failed to get students excited about learning?

Most profiles of the kind reported herein, however, need to be viewed with some caution. These kinds of statistical summaries, while useful, often fail to provide a balanced picture. The academic achievement profile of African-American youngsters just presented, for example, says little about those youngsters who are in fact succeeding academically. Many of these youngsters are reared in the same environment within which many of their African-American peers are failing, yet some are succeeding at rates equal to, if not in excess of, their White peers. What factors contribute to the differential academic success rates of African-American youngsters, given that all of them are essentially products of the same environment? Perhaps an understanding of the correlates of achievement might provide us with an answer to these questions. Parham and Parham (1989) have identified four correlates of achievement that they feel are key to the academic survival of African-American youth.

CORRELATES OF ACHIEVEMENT

Identifying the correlates of positive and negative achievement for the African-American youngster has been the focus of several investigations. The list of factors that potentially correlate with (either positive or negative) academic achievement is almost endless. Yet several factors are more consistently identified as contributing to or inhibiting academic achievement in Black youngsters. Parham and Parham (1989) have suggested that these factors include self-concept, value orientation, teacher expectation, and family composition.

BLACK SELF-CONCEPT

A variable that undoubtedly influences the achievement aspirations of Black youngsters is self-concept. Yet asking exactly how self-concept impacts achievement aspirations yields debatable answers. Psychologists and sociologists have argued that the self is found to be in direct relation to how a person thinks others perceive him or her (Rogers, 1961). Thus, a person in our society validates his or her identity through the evaluations of significant others. If the notion of necessary external validation is accurate, it seems reasonable to assume that the achievement aspirations of Black youngsters would be influenced by evaluations by significant others in the child's life.

While such an assertion might be reasonable, researchers have had difficulty agreeing on where the child's source of validation is derived. Some research suggests that validation and approval are derived from the Black community (Banks, 1972; Barnes, 1972; Norton, 1983). Unfortunately, the larger body of research suggests that approval is sought from the dominant White culture (Kardiner and Ovessey, 1951, 1968); and, because of the negative attitudes perpetuated by the larger White society, positive achievement by Blacks was not an unexpected outcome.

Investigations of the Black self-concept and self-esteem have generally assumed that every aspect of Black life is a reflection of the group's caste-like position in the dominant society, and that Black Americans are incapable of rejecting the negativistic images of themselves perpetuated by the dominant White society. The prototype for these studies was presented by Clark and Clark (1947) in an investigation in which they found that Black children preferred White dolls to Black dolls. They concluded that the children's choice of White dolls was a reflection of their group self-hatred. Other studies followed (Goodman, 1952; Moreland, 1958) which similarly pointed out the tendency for Black children to identify with and/or prefer White skin, White dolls, and White friends. These identity problems, the literature suggested, were linked to problems of self-evaluation. In addition, the literature further pointed out that Black people's assignment to second-class status, together with White racists' insistence on Black people's innate inferiority, no doubt was instrumental in creating doubts in Black people concerning their own worth (Arnaz, 1972).

Several authors have sought to explain this self-hate phenomenon by hypothesizing that Black people's hostility towards the oppressor was so threatening that repression of hostile feelings was the only means by which they could deal with their feelings (Kardiner & Ovessey, 1968). In turn, the repressed hostility was redirected internally and thus stimulated self-hatred. Other attempts were made to explain Black self-hatred by pointing out Black people's simultaneous feelings of hatred of oppressors and desires to imitate them, thus resulting in feelings of self-hate, confused identity, and the like (Kardiner & Ovessey, 1951). It was, in fact, Kardiner and Ovessey (1951, p. 297) who clearly exemplified this negative analysis of Black subgroup status when they asserted,

> the Negro has no possible basis for a healthy self-esteem and every incentive for self-hatred. The basic fact is that the Negro's aspiration level, good conscience, and even good performance are irrelevant in face of the glaring fact that the Negro gets a poor reflection of himself in the behavior of Whites, no matter what he does, or what his merits are. The chief distinguishing factor in the Negro is that he must identify himself with the Negro, but this initiates the compensatory identification with the White (person) who is also hated.

Dansby (1972) suggested that an example of this "identification with the aggressor" or imitation of Whites could be seen in Black people's use of cosmetic products to make themselves appear White (i.e., straightening hair, lightening skin tones, etc.). In addition to these behavioral examples, the literature was replete with studies describing the phenomenon of identifying with the oppressor. Bayton et al. (1956) described minority group persons as tending to idealize the majority group, thus contributing to their own self-rejection. Also, Pettigrew (1974) cited a large body of psychological literature that demonstrated the power of role playing on conceptions of self. He postulated that Blacks had played the role of "stupid," "slow," and "inferior" to appease the White power structure to the detriment of their own self-esteem and integrity.

Wyne (1974) has also addressed the consequences of this role-playing behavior. He asserted that, when the minority tends to use the majority as an emulative reference group (as Blacks have done), the result is usually that the minority tends to adopt those behaviors and beliefs about the self that they feel the majority holds to be desirable. Wyne concluded that the effect becomes a self-fulfilling prophecy, reinforcing the prejudiced feelings and beliefs of the majority.

What might be added to the observations by Pettigrew (1964) and Wyne (1974), however, is the possibility that such role playing may also hinder attempts by researchers to perceive, understand, and/or interpret the nature of Black self-concept. Both authors seem to suggest that Black people have often felt it necessary to conceal their true selves in order to survive in a racist social order. Ames (1950) speaks to this phenomenon of "role playing" or "mask wearing" as he states, "...got one mind for White folks to see; another for what I know is me." While explanations and observations of this tendency to disguise oneself appear less frequently in the literature, they do provide additional data through which to evaluate studies on the Black self.

As the preceding studies indicate, it was common for White and Black social scientists to write and reiterate that Black people, in general, have had a negative self-concept. Furthermore, these tendencies towards negative self-conceptions have been linked to such phenomena as identification with the aggressor, over-assimilation, and low achievement.

In contrast to the low-self-concept/low-achievement-oriented studies of the past, more contemporary research cites evidence that African-American children do have positive racial self-concepts (Powell & Fuller, 1970). In fact, Powell (1983) concludes that the concept of low self-esteem in Black children should be discarded in light of several extensive literature reviews (Wylie, 1978; Rosenberg, 1979; Weinberg, 1977), which revealed (a) little or no differences in self-concept between Black and White children, and (b) higher self-esteem scores in Black children.

The low self-concept conclusion of the past has also been questioned by challenging the notion that Black children agree

with and internalize the negative evaluations of them promoted by the larger society. On the contrary, several studies
have indicated that African-American children do not believe
or agree with negative stereotypes about themselves or that
they are inferior (Brigham, 1974; Campbell, 1976; Rosenberg,
1979). According to Gurin & Epps (1975) what has been over-
looked is the minimization of the role of the oppressor (in
influencing self-images), and more specifically, the adaptive
strengths of the African-American (child). Consequently, social scientists, teachers, and students themselves must come
to grips with the fact that positive academic achievement
among Black children is not only a possibility, but a realistic
expectation.

   While the debate over the disposition of the Black child's
self-concept may be temporarily suspended, the notion that a
child's sense of self influences his or her academic achievement appears to be unanimous. If such is the case, how can the
community contribute to the development of a healthy self-
image? We believe that parents and immediate family must
provide reinforcement for a child's self-image by instilling a
sense of pride, and by acting as a filter for the negative images
a child is exposed to. Parents and schools must play a role in
communicating both expectations and encouragement for
achievement, along with constant praise and reinforcement
for a child's mastery of various developmental and educational tasks. Children must also be assisted in identifying and
participating in positive peer relationships and group activities that reinforce a positive sense of self.

   Each of these influences, together with other community
resources (churches, parks and recreation areas, business
leaders) must collaborate to reinforce for the African-American child principles of self-affirmation and self-determination.

   Other suggestions for enhancing self-concept were provided by Powell (1982) in her study on the effects of school
desegration on the self-concepts of Black children. Her inves-

tigation concluded that, in order for self-concept of children in various schools to develop in a normal pattern, several criteria seem to be necessary. Those factors included:

- Maximum participation by parents and teachers
- Mores and values of the home reinforced in the immediate community and school
- Black culture and life styles reflected in the educational curriculum
- Academic achievement being encouraged regardless of social class

VALUE ORIENTATION
AS A CORRELATE

Thomas (1967) defines values as normative, conceptual standards of desired behavior that influence individuals in choosing among personally perceived alternative behavior. Values are believed to influence ways in which people think, feel, and behave (Kluckjohn and Strodtbeck, 1961). As such, values may also influence academic achievement of Black youngsters. Much of what a Black youngster comes to value positively and negatively in the world is influenced by what significant others in their life value as well. Typically, values of specific ethnic groups are transmitted from generation to generation in ways that allow cultural traditions to continue and self-actualizing behavior to flourish. Occasionally, however, perceptions that culture-specific values are less functional than values of other cultures force many Black youngsters to abandon traditional African-American values in favor of Euro-centric ones. One consequence of this phenomenon is the adoption of many behaviors that are perceived as functional, but that ultimately prove to be self-destructive to the individual and the community. Nobles (1980, 1986) helps to clarify the relationships between personal values and academic achievement by suggesting that ideas are the substance of behavior. Essentially, Nobles implies that the development of a strong desire to achieve academically, along with behavior directed toward that goal attainment, is facilitated by a conceptual grounding in the philosophies of African culture.

The notion that education is a necessity for survival and advancement of one's people and oneself is a value that must be promoted by significant others in the child's life. We believe that academic achievement in Black youngsters occurs when achievement is encouraged and supported by the community at large. Families, schools, churches, community organizations, and peer groups must come together in a collective voice and support efforts towards excellence.

In the absence of a unanimous consent for this idea, there must be enough support from particular significant others in the child's life, in order for that value to be internalized and practiced by the youngster.

The present authors would also argue that academic achievement is stifled when motivation to achieve is nonexistent and the desire to achieve is challenged by environmental obstacles preventing goal attainment. If the Black community is to be the reference point around which Black youngsters seek validation and support, then the community must also accept the challenge of eliminating the barriers that prevent Black youth from achieving academically. Ironically, the very institutions that are supposed to encourage achievement are the ones that hinder it. Nowhere is this example clearer than in some of our schools.

Primary and secondary educational institutions have become havens for drug abuse, gang violence, extortion, and misconduct. As stated earlier, many youngsters are more concerned with mastering the intricacies of selling drugs for profit than they are about learning the intricacies of reading, writing, and counting. The idea of making large sums of money without much work proves to be a powerful distractor to many youth. Clearly, there is a deterioration of African values when the attainment of wealth and material posses-sions at any cost are valued over the uplifting of one's people.

However, many youngsters emerge from what is per-ceived to be negative environments, with the determination to succeed in life's endeavors despite less than ideal circum-stances. We believe that youngsters who make it, and who are successful in achieving academically, manage to remain fo-cused on an ideal of self-determination. They develop the will and intent to succeed in spite of negative elements and seem-ingly insurmountable obstacles in the environment. Indeed, it is the child him- or herself who must commit to excellence over destructive distractions. Having said this, however, we recog-nize that individual choices are influenced by elements in the environment that shape the way our children process infor-mation and make sense of their world.

Kunjufu (1986) suggests that values are the foundation for motivation, which in turn influences one's behavior. He further asserts that values are developed and nurtured through exposure to information. If Kunjufu's assertion is at all correct (and we suspect it is), then some analysis of the types of information our children are receiving (or not re-ceiving) is in order, and may help to crystalize how incor-poration of values influence achievement of Black youngsters.

Exposure to massive amounts of television on a daily basis has been identified as one of the prime socializers of African-American youngsters. In subtle and some not so sub-tle ways, our children's value systems are being influenced and shaped by what they visually and auditorily absorb from that medium (Berry, 1982). This realization is compounded by the notion that Black children devote a disproportionately high amount of time to television viewing (as high as six hours per day) and, like other children, are likely to believe that television accurately reflects life as it really is or should be (Greenberg & Dervin, 1970). Berry (1982) helps to further clarify the question of television's influence on the development of values and the desire to achieve by asking two questions. First:

> Television depicts levels of academic and occupational attainment. To what extend does television convey to African-American children the concept that they can be successful only in a (Black) environment; and to what extent must aspiration for broader occupational and academic positions in a multi-cultural world be limited? Second:

> Television occupies a prestigious position in our society, and for some young people, it tends to validate and add glamour to the roles being played. To what extent are children patterning their behavior and establishing personal attitudes (and values) from television characters who may not be wholesome role models?...

Children are being exposed to images and role models that depict the Black community in very negative ways. Images of street smart children and adults who will do whatever it takes to "get over" (lie, cheat, steal, murder, sell narcotics) are very inappropriate. Images of Blacks being confined to low-status jobs, as well as being prevented from exploring a wider variety of career options, are also inappropriate and may be especially damaging to a child's achievement aspirations. Scenarios that promote money, status, material possessions, and sexual exploits as measures of manhood and womanhood are also extremely destructive.

In many cases, the Black community has reacted strongly to these negative portrayals of Blacks on television by calling for a change of venue. Yet the very community demanding that television images change fails to realize that the validation for our children adopting these negative stereotypes and portrayals are being provided in and by the community itself. Street corners are filled with dozens of individuals who have simply given up on life, and who feel helpless to change their condition.

Parents also fail to support their children in their educational pursuits in a number of ways. Among those are:

- Failure to review lessons with children who are completing homework assignments
- Failure to insist that homework be completed before engaging in any extracurricular activities (including television)
- Failure to articulate parental expectations regarding their child's academic performance to the teacher and insisting on periodic reviews
- Failure to provide guidance when viewing television programming with their children

If exposure to information is to remain a prominent influence on values, and if values are in turn to influence behavior, then manipulating the type, amount, and quality of information our children receive will help them to develop a value system that is more consistent with their African culture. Such values might include, for example, the principles of Nguzo Saba (Karenga, 1976). These include:

Umoja	Unity
Kujichagulia	Self-determination
Ujima	Collective work and responsibility
Ujamaa	Cooperative economics
Nia	Purpose
Kuumba	Creativity
Imani	Faith

Presentation of, and teaching about Afro-centric value systems may be an important strategy in helping our children to develop the will and intent to achieve.

TEACHER EXPECTATIONS AS A CORRELATE

Teacher expectations are yet another correlate of academic achievement, which spawned widespread interest among researchers. The bulk of the studies suggesting that teacher attitudes and expectations affect a child's school performance began to appear in the late 1960s and early 1970s when Rosenthal and Jacobson published their now classic study, *Pygmalion in the Classroom* (1968).

At the heart of the Rosenthal and Jacobson experiment was a belief that teacher's expectations would significantly affect the learning of a group of normally distributed, socially and racially mixed elementary school children, when their teachers were told the children possessed special intellectual talents. The teachers were also told that these "talented" children would show marked intellectual improvement by the end of the first few months of the experiment. The results confirmed the experimenter's prediction in that these intellectually talented students scored significantly higher than the control group on measures of IQ.

In explaining their results, Rosenthal and Jacobson speculated that teachers are especially attentive to students who are expected to show intellectual promise. These students are often treated in a more encouraging manner, and teachers tend to show increased tolerance and patience with the child's learning process. The converse is true for students perceived to be less intellectually gifted: When students are not expected to make significant educational gains, then less attention and encouragement are given to them.

Several other studies (Beez, 1968; Palardy, 1969; Pidgeon, 1970; Rothbart, Dalfen & Barrett, 1971; Rubovitz & Maehr, 1973), all documenting the teacher expectancy effect, came on the heels of the heralded Pygmalion experiment. In a study conducted by Beez (1968), for example, faked psychological dossiers, describing "high-ability" preschool students in favorable terms and "lower-ability" preschool students in less favorable terms, were given to teachers who worked with these "high-" and "low-ability" preschoolers on simple word learning tasks. As predicted, high-ability preschool students learned more words than their presumably low-ability peers. This differential in performance among the preschool students, according to Beez, was attributable to, at least in part, the expectations of the students held by teachers of both groups.

Palardy's (1969) study examined the differential perceptions of teachers and wondered what effect these perceptions would have on boys and girls learning how to read. Despite every child receiving above-average reading pretest scores, when boys were taught by teachers who perceived their ability to learn to be as good as girls, boys learned as well as girls. When taught by teachers who perceived their ability to learn to be lower than girls, boys were outperformed by girls.

The Rubovitz and Maehr (1973) investigation took a slightly different slant in that differential teacher expectations with respect to student's race and learning ability were of interest. A group of four mixed-ability eighth-grade students (two African-Americans and two Anglos) were assigned to one of 66 women teachers (creating 66 teacher-student groupings), and two of the four students in each group (one African-American and one Anglo) were randomly given high IQ scores. The experimenters found differential teacher expectancy effects in predicted and unpredicted directions, and the student's race proved to be a salient factor. African-Americans, both gifted and nongifted received less favorable treatment than gifted and nongifted Anglos. In rank order, increased attention and encouragement were given to gifted Anglos, nongifted Anglos, nongifted African-Americans, and gifted African-Americans. In essence, African-American giftedness was penalized with less attention and praise, whereas Anglo giftedness was rewarded.

By way of balance, it should be pointed out, however, that not all teacher expectancy studies resulted in a finding consistent with these investigations. The Claiborn (1969) and Fleming and Anttonen (1971) studies are cases in point. Both involved the usual teacher-student grouping, and expectations of students' intellectual talent (or lack thereof) were shaped using fake data. Post-test results in both studies failed to show greater relative gains in learning between experimental and control groups.

FAMILY BACKGROUND
AS A CORRELATE

Historically, many social scientists have attempted to answer the question of academic achievement in Black youngsters by assuming that the environment negatively impacted the child. That is, it was assumed that low achievement was related to an absence of supportive attributes external to the child him/herself. The chief scapegoat in these studies appeared to have been the family.

As early as the 1930s, research sought to document the consequences of poverty on the perceived instability, weakness, and disintegration of the family (Frazier, 1939). Not surprisingly, much of the subsequent research attempted to validate these prior assumptions about the pathological Black family (Moynihan, 1965; Rainwater, 1966). Moynihan (1965), for example, characterizes the family as "tangle and web of pathology."

Similarly, Rainwater (1966) suggested that the functional autonomy of the Black family reflected destructive features that expressed themselves in violent, repressive, and depraved life styles. These studies went on to further suggest that this disorganized family contributed to personality, social, cognitive, and mental deficits in Black children.

By and large, the family variables identified as culprits included low SES, a matriarchal family structure, and a lack of educational resources (Clark, 1983). Assuming these factors are absolutely essential in promoting academic achievement in some youngsters, perceived low achievement by Blacks came as no surprise.

Explaining positive achievement of Black youth who are nurtured in a supportive environment has been a recent, albeit infrequent focus in the literature. For one thing, crediting the Black family (supportive or not) with helping to develop and promote achievement ideals occurs on too few fronts.

Images of the pathological and disorganized family have begun to change over the past decade, however. In some respects the formation of positive family images has been assisted by researchers who understood that previous characterizations of the unhealthy Black family were in part influenced by biased assumptions and conclusions of the previous researchers themselves. Not surprisingly, then, these latest studies (Billingsley, 1968; Hill, 1971; Ladner, 1975; Stack, 1973) have served as a reaction to previous Black family research by criticizing previous research efforts, and by attempting to explain family dynamics and composition in a way that highlights strengths of the family. For example, Billingsley (1968) cautions researchers against classifying the "Black family" as a single entity, rather than recognizing that, indeed, no "one" description accurately characterizes the Black family of today. Similarly, Hill (1971) presented strengths or factors that have helped Black families to sustain themselves under less than ideal circumstances. These include strong orientations to work, religion, achievement, strong kinship bonds, and role flexibility by family members.

Recent studies on the Black family have continued to substantiate the work by Billingsley, Hill, and Ladner, by isolating the factors that help modern Black family members in meeting their needs (McAdoo, 1986; Nobles, 1986). While successful in characterizing the Black family as a vehicle that presumably helps to foster academic achievement in Black youth, these studies have been limited in their ability to explain exactly how achievement is supported and encouraged.

The most important study to emerge in the literature that attempts to explain this phenomenon was conducted by Clark (1983). Clark attempted to answer the question of "why poor Black children succeed or fail" in his book *Family Life and School Achievement*. Essentially, he compares and contrasts five high achieving with five low achieving students, and identifies parenting and child development strategies used by each family. He concludes that parents' dispositions and interpersonal relationships with the child are the main contributors to a child's success in school. Perhaps the most profound statement made in Clark's research effort is that communication and quality of interaction are more important than sociodemographic variables (i.e., family composition, income status) in predicting high achievement in Black youngsters. However, it is our contention that, while quality of interaction between parent and child is an important component in school achievement, we cannot overlook a youngster's willingness and motivation to respond to supportive environmental cues. Indeed, motivation is a characteristic that emerges from within the child itself.

EDUCATIONAL CHALLENGES FOR THE 1990s

We have attempted to point out in this chapter that the academic achievement of African-American youngsters, generally speaking, has been less than satisfactory. If one looks at the data presented and concludes that educational and academic achievement is a hopeless enterprise, then the future of African-American educational achievement is bleak indeed. If, however, one views the data with concern and uses it is an opportunity to make a difference, then several challenges face school systems, the Black community, and indeed the students themselves as we move into the 1990s.

First, the question of role definition requires all of us to ask ourselves whether we define our roles as educators in terms of function or in terms of students' needs. Defining our roles in terms of function relegates us to certain activities (lecture, answering questions, office hours, grading tests). Defining our roles in terms of needs of students requires that educators become a barometer of student needs such that one learns to translate student needs into social change.

Educators may also have to assist parents and provide them with some feedback on how best to support the intellectual growth and development of their children. Such feedback might help parents avoid behaviors and/or attitudes that are less than supportive of children's academic achievement.

Educators must also help parents to understand, as Reginald Clark (1983) points out in *Family Life and School Achievement*, that there is a strong correlation between family expectations for youngsters and those youngsters' being high achievers. The four parental dispositions observed by Clark include:

1. Parents' willingness to put their children's growth and development above their own.
2. Parents who believe that schools cannot do and teach everything to their children; consequently, parents take personal responsibility for assisting their children in developing skills needed for success in the classroom.
3. Parents who believe that children are personally responsible for pursuing knowledge and consequently expect regular classroom attendance and active participation in classroom activities. Such a practice also provides parents with a daily monitor of a child's academic progress.
4. Parents who routinely emphasize that their children should exceed their own goal attainment, and even consider pursuing secondary training beyond that which they personally received. Active involvement by parents is not only beneficial to a child's cognitive growth, involvement also helps to strengthen the emotional bond between parent and child.

Educators also need to consider the notion that learning is best when it is additive in nature (White, 1984). As teachers and educators, we must all become assessors of talent and skills, build on them, and be able to adapt one's content to a mode in which the student learns best. The children that we teach and counsel in the classroom are very bright, but they require our interest and stimulation. If children can learn the words to a song, "I Need Love" by L.L. Kool-J.,[2] they can certainly learn the writings of Carter G. Woodson about the miseducation of the Negro. If they can learn the words to "Au Casanova,"[3] they can certainly learn the principles of Martin Luther King's book, *Strength to Love*. If children can memorize the words to Gregory Abbott's hit tune, "Shake You Down,"[4] or the words to Michael Jackson's hit song, "Bad,"[5] certainly they can learn the principles of self-pride and self-determination as taught by Marcus Garvey and Elijah Muhammad.

It is also important for educators to accept the challenge of making their curriculum more culturally relevant. Exposure to history, culture, heros, and symbols helps students believe in the possibilities and potentialities for them to achieve. Once a year cultural programming is a good start, but far from sufficient. Textbooks and curriculum guides that are used everyday in the classroom should, at a minimum, contain figures that mirror the experiences of Black students in their communities.

Educators must also recognize that motivation to learn is enhanced when students see the need, relevance, and reason for each lesson they learn. As such, one of the most effective ways we know of teaching education and curriculum is teaching content through problem solving. Thus, educators should be encouraged to design their lesson plans around resolving contemporary issues that students must confront in their day-to-day lives.

Finally, teachers and counselors must help our youth to master the developmental task of identity development, and find ways to enhance our children's self-esteem. These are crucial elements in helping our children work through issues of:

1. Worrying too much about what other people think.
2. Fear of failure.
3. Low frustration tolerance.
4. Always blaming someone else for their lack of success.

Indeed, helping them to develop a sense of self-determination is another key to reducing their at-risk status.

CHAPTER SIX

MENTAL HEALTH SERVICE DELIVERY

In recent years, our nation has witnessed an increasing demand for psychotherapeutic services. This demand, in part, is fueled by personal needs for seeking greater self-actualization. However, much of this demand has been generated by individuals who are experiencing mild to extreme difficulties in adjusting to a complex environment, which is constantly in the process of change. Simultaneously, there is also a move to deliver a more effective service to ethnic populations in general and to African-Americans in particular who, because of oppressive and social/environmental realities, experience extreme personal stress and tension when compared to other groups.

The purpose of this chapter, then, is to discuss the general issues as they relate to mental health in the Black community. Our discussion will begin by exploring the questions of, "What is mental health?" and "How is mental health operationalized in the Black community?" The chapter will continue with discussions about therapeutic prognosis, help-seeking behaviors in African-Americans, and the dynamics and therapy involved in working with an African-American client. This chapter will conclude with a brief discussion of training issues as they relate to mental health professionals delivering service to African-American clients.

MENTAL HEALTH
OR MENTAL ILLNESS:
A QUESTION OF PERSPECTIVE

There is considerable disagreement regarding what constitutes mental health and/or mental illness. Most mental health professionals, however, generally assume that a state of mental health exists when individuals are mentally free of the psychological ailments and/or distortions that negatively affect cognitive, emotional, and behavioral abilities, or that in some way impede an individual's growth and ability to reach full potential (that is, when one feels his or her life has moved, is moving, or has the potential to move in a meaningful direction).

In the first edition of *The Psychology of Blacks*, White (1984) discusses the notion of mental health for Black people. Among other things, he concluded that psychologically healthy Black persons are those who interpret the Afro-American ethos into their own life space, are psychologically open to self and able to relate to others, are resourceful, inventive, imaginative, and enterprising in their approach to life. White also contends that mental health for Blacks requires that a person be centered in, grounded in, or otherwise in touch with one's African-American makeup.

The importance of White's assertion is underscored by the assumption that what constitutes mental health for Blacks needs to be understood in the context of one's own culture. Traditionally, Euro-centric standards of what constitutes mental health are often inappropriate for Blacks because they are based on the philosophies, values, and mores of Euro-American culture, and they use these variables to develop normative standards of mental health based only on Euro-American culture. Thus, what constitutes sane or insane behavior, mental health or mental illness, or normal or abnormal behavior is always in relation to a White normative standard.

In recent years, African-American scholars have begun to articulate their own definitions of what constitutes mental health and self-actualizing behavior for African-American people. These models are based more on an Afro-centric view of mental health and mental illness, and are more accurate indicators of normal and/or abnormal behavior in Black people.

Parham and Helms (1985), for example, examine the relationship between a Black person's racial identity attitudes and his/her mentally healthy, self-actualizing behaviors. Generally, the results suggest that the development of pro-Black attitudes may be indicative of healthy psychological adjustment, whereas attitudes that denigrate one's self as a Black person while simultaneously promoting wishes to be White may be psychologically maladaptive.

In a similar context, other researchers have suggested that there are boundaries defining certain behaviors as psychologically healthy and other behaviors as psychologically unhealthy. For example, Pugh (1972) viewed behaviors such as over-assimilation, the wanting-to-be-like-White attitude, and identification with the aggressor/oppressor as unhealthy psychological defensive mechanisms. Other scholars have also asserted that tough attitudes and behaviors such as color denial (Myers and Yochelson, 1949), identification with the White caste (Adams, 1950), and dependence on White society for self-definition (Thomas, 1971) may act as a defense against generalized anxiety; they are nonetheless psychologically unhealthy. These authors seem to suggest that the adoption of attitudes and behaviors by Blacks, which are similar to those described by Pugh (1972), is tantamount to the development of neurotic tendencies because such behaviors distort or stunt growth toward self-actualization, enhance self-defeating tendencies, and diminish the capacity to be a complete human being (Thomas, 1971). In contrast to negative, self-defeating behaviors related to being Black, other authors assert that pro-Black attitudes and behaviors may be indicative of positive psychological functioning (Hilliard, 1972; Williams, 1981; Thomas, 1971; Carter and Helms, 1984; Nobles, 1986; Baldwin, 1984).

Another attempt to define mental health from an Afrocentric perspective suggests that, rather than classify behaviors as mentally healthy or mentally ill, behaviors should be classified as ordered or disordered (Akbar, 1981). According to Akbar (1981), ordered behavior is described as a naturally disposed tendency to maintain life and perpetuate one's self. Thus, behaviors that foster, cultivate, and promote the survival of one's self and one's people are seen as psychologically ordered. In contrast, disordered behavior impedes or hinders survival of the organism or threatens the maintenance of life and the growth of an individual.

In discussing his concept of ordered and disordered behavior, Akbar (1981) further proposes a classification system of disorders among African-Americans that result from being an oppressed group. His classification of disorders assumes that oppression is an unnatural and inhuman phenomenon that stimulates unnatural human behavior. Akbar's classification system includes:

> *Alien Self-disorder:* Individuals who have been socialized to be other than themselves, and whose very lives and life styles represent a rejection of their natural African dispositions.
>
> *Antiself Disorder:* Individuals who, in addition to being socialized to be other than themselves, identify with the projected hostility and negativism towards his or her group of origin.
>
> *Self-destructive Disorder:* Individuals who engage in self-defeating attempts to survive in a society that systematically frustrates normal efforts for natural human growth; out of an urgency for survival, these individuals have chosen personally and socially destructive ways to alleviate immediate wants, despite the fact that these ways are often destructive and detrimental to one's self and one's community.
>
> *Organic Disorder:* Individuals afflicted with conditions that are the result of physiological, neurological, or biochemical malfunction.

What implications, then, do these studies and classification systems have for psychologists and therapists who work with Black clients in therapy? Personality theories of African-Americans, especially those articulated by Nobles (1986), Akbar (1981), Baldwin (1984), Azibo (1983), and Parham and Helms (1985), stress the necessity of achieving congruence between the "self" one wishes to become, and one's true African-American makeup if one is to be a fully functioning and well-adjusted individual. If there is an aspect or factor of personality that does not fit well with, function well with, or contribute constructively to the overall personality organization, then the efficient functioning of the personality is decreased or perhaps even seriously disrupted. Thus, attitudes and behaviors that devalue Blackness, or that over-assimilate White culture values, and the like, can be seen as representing degrees of incongruence between a Black person's real self and idealized self because they violate the natural order of that person's African makeup.

If one assumes that nonself-actualizing behavior is related to the degree of incongruence between one's real self and idealized self (Rogers, 1961; Nobles, 1986), it is likely that therapists and psychologists will see different degrees of psychological neurosis related to clients who display varying degrees of racial identity attitudes. As such, service providers may need to assist clients with achieving some sense of integration or congruence between the real self and the idealized self. In doing so, therapists will need to deal with their clients' past experiences that have shaped their perceptions in a disordered fashion, as well as the stress surrounding such experiences. Service providers may also need to assist clients in analyzing their behaviors that hinder, threaten, or impede their growth as human organisms. Service providers may also want to assist clients in becoming more comfortable with themselves as African-American persons, while helping them to identify their resistance to more positive Black perspectives.

Such efforts might include a thorough examination of a client's self-esteem or self-worth.

THERAPEUTIC PROGNOSIS: CONTRADICTORY FINDINGS

If one attempts to gain a historical overview of mental illness as it relates to Black populations, an examination of the literature will readily reveal that Blacks are perceived to be more prone to psychological disorders than Whites, and characteristically have higher rates of mental diseases. However, a closer look at the research reveals that, although extensive in scope, the literature is often contradictory in its findings. Furthermore, it is clear that many investigations have made gross generalizations from their data and/or biased their data with a priori assumptions (Thomas and Sillen, 1972). While the scope of this chapter limits the time we can devote to this topic, mention should be made of an excellent review article (Fisher, 1969) that, while nearly twenty years old, has much contemporary relevance.

Fisher reviews the literature on mental illness in Blacks and cites several problems with the research. The first has to do with the conceptualization of the problem, and the fact that service providers employ a different frame of reference than their clients. Ultimately, what emerges as mentally ill or not depends upon how one defines mental illness and the definer's frame of reference. More recent reviews continue to show that Blacks are often stereotyped in the psychiatric literature as not being psychologically minded, and as lacking the psychological sophistication and motivation necessary for successful psychotherapy. Thus Blacks are viewed as having a primitive character structure, and as being too jovial to be depressed and too impoverished to experience objective loss (Adebimpe, 1981). This tendency to misdiagnose and over-diagnose severe psychopathology has persisted despite the awareness of social-cultural differences between Blacks and Whites brought about by the Black Revolution (King, 1978). Even in contemporary service delivery, Adebimpe (1981) was quick to recognize that Black patients run a higher risk of being misdiagnosed as schizophrenics, whereas White patients showing identical behaviors are more likely to receive diagnoses as depressed.

Fisher (1969) discusses other issues. One has to do with the fact that, statistically, mental illness is sometimes defined according to whether persons are admitted to treatment. Fisher then cites research suggesting that, in some cases, Blacks are admitted to hospitals faster than Whites. He also addresses the fact that most research on race or mental illness historically uses state facilities for subject pools. Therefore, one would expect an uneven distribution of Black and other low-SES populations in state compared with private facilities. A final issue has to do with the fact that assessment of illness rates is also measured by incidence (number of new cases) and prevalence (total number of cases present in a population at a given time). Therefore, since there are significantly higher numbers of Blacks in state hospitals and research samples are taken from state hospitals, obvious biases result when you use incidence and prevalence data from those institutions for assessing mental illness. These biased samples then have been used to make generalizations about Black people as a whole.

Another interesting analysis related to Black people in the process of therapy was written by Block (1980). Block suggests that the status of Black people in psychotherapy can be understood via several trends. The first trend, which spans the first half of this century, indicates that Blacks were depicted as persons limited in cognitive, emotional, and social abilities who were (or should be) content with their low status because of their relative immaturity compared to the dominant White culture (Thomas and Sillen, 1972). This emphasis on immaturity and innate limited abilities led White clinicians and other researchers to diagnose higher rates of hysteria and impulse character disorders among Blacks. The second trend discussed by Block began to take shape around the end of World War II when large numbers of Black servicemen were being treated by White psychiatrists. The psychological literature then began to focus on their suspicion, hostility, and distrust of White therapists and their preoccupation with discussing racial issues during therapy sessions. These characteristics, according to Block, were interpreted either as resistance or as manifestations of early psychotic processes with diagnoses such as incipient paranoia, uncontrolled aggressive reactions, and chronic schizophrenia being assigned to those Black patients. The third trend began to take shape during and after the Civil Rights/Black Power era when the psychological literature on Blacks shifted to an acceptance of the need for Blacks to develop different defensive coping styles to handle their environmental realities. Racial consciousness, anger, and distrust could now be viewed as appropriate, adaptive behavior (Grier and Cobbs, 1968), particularly since such characteristics were being proposed and validated by Black and other minority psychologists. Regardless of whether or not these characteristics were seen as normal or abnormal, the assignment of these particular descriptors to Black patients made them poor candidates for psychotherapy in the eyes of many White clinicians.

From time to time, we ask our students to detail for us what characteristics they would like to find in their "ideal" patient whom they might see in therapy. Whether we sample graduate or undergraduate students, or even some professionals, we begin to see a similar pattern. The characteristics most highly valued in clients include:

1. Intelligent.
2. Motivated.

3. Verbal.
4. Attractive.
5. Able to pay.
6. Articulate.
7. Personable.
8. Trusting.
9. Disclosive.

Once this list was generated, students and other people sampled readily agreed that these are the characteristics of their "ideal" client. We then asked our respondents to examine the psychological literature as well as generic societal stereotypes in an attempt to ascertain the degree of congruence (correlation) between characteristics most highly valued in typical clients and those stereotypically associated with persons from different ethnic groups. Figure 6.1 presents an illustration of how closely Black clients are perceived to mirror those qualities most highly valued in "ideal clients," particularly when compared to their White counterparts. The figure accurately illustrates how closely therapeutic stereotypes of typical White clients match those characteristics most highly valued in ideal client populations. Conversely, the figure is equally clear in illustrating how stereotypic attitudes of Black clients conflict with the "ideal client" characteristics. Based on these generalizations and the characteristic portrayals of Blacks, many Black patients were assumed to be poor candidates for psychotherapy. Stereotypic presentations of Black clients set the tone for stereotypic treatment of Blacks. If Black patients continue to be characterized as being less verbal, impulse-ridden, more concrete than abstract in thought, and having difficulty dealing with intrapsychic material, therapists might be encouraged to adopt more action-oriented, compared with insight-oriented, therapeutic strategies when working with Black patients (Kincaid, 1968; Smith, 1977).

FIGURE 6.1.

PERCEIVED CHARACTERISTICS OF WHITE MIDDLE CLASS	TYPICAL CHARACTERISTICS VALUED IN CLIENTS	PERCEIVED CHARACTERISTICS OF BLACKS
Verbal	Introspetion	Nonintrospective
Intelligent	Motivation	Emotionally Immature
Motivated	Emotionally Controlled	Unmotivated
Delay of gratification	Trusting	Impulse-Ridden
Trusting	Able to Disclose	Suspicious
Disclosive	Highly Verbal	Angry/Hostile
Introspective	Intelligent	Not Articulate
		Nonself-Disclosive
		Low Intelligence

PROGNOSIS-POTENTIAL TO BENEFIT FROM PSYCHOTHERAPY

GOOD

POOR

119

HELP SEEKING BEHAVIORS
IN AFRICAN-AMERICANS

Contemporary service delivery models, in some respects, represent a shift away from hospitalization and institutionalization to more outpatient and community mental health center facilities. Despite this shift, Black patients/clients are still under-represented and under-served. This suggests that the majority of Black persons needing some type of psychological care are not receiving such. Furthermore, of those who begin treatment, better than 50 percent of those discontinue treatment after the initial session (Sue, 1977). While several factors are cited for this alarming statistic, diagnosis and treatment by non-Black therapists are often implicated. Other factors include differential expectations between clients and therapists, and service by paraprofessional rather than professional workers.

Examination of literature suggested by and large that therapy or counseling has not been adequately utilized by Black people to deal with their problems. In fact, Black people are more likely to rely on traditional support networks (relatives, grandmothers, ministers) during times of stress, anxiety, and tension.

If, however, a Black person makes a decision to utilize psychotherapeutic services, it is likely that several factors are involved. Block (1980) discusses these issues sufficiently. The first is an extreme willingness on the part of African-American people to take a risk with the mental health system despite a negative history of Blacks with respect to the delivery of psychological services. It is also probable that, since African-Americans may initially utilize traditional support networks in times of stress, these traditional support systems are not functioning effectively for the individual, either because of unavailability or because the person chooses not to use them. Consequently, service providers may see clients who are more debilitated since the amount of time between the presenting problem and therapeutic intervention is apt to be longer.

There is also the possibility that a Black client may display a greater sense of fear and suspiciousness. These feelings are stimulated not only by the prospect of therapy itself, but also by the possibility and probability of working with a non-Black professional, and having to entrust one's life stories and pain to a non-Black person. It is also likely that persons seeking therapeutic services may be partially to well educated since these individuals tend to have a better understanding for and trust in traditional psychological services. It is also probable that the children and adolescents who are seen in mental health clinics in community facilities may be referrals from two primary sources: the courts and schools. If such is the case, a clinician can expect to encounter a heightened sense of resistance, suspiciousness, and even hostility from the patient related to what may possibly be a mandated participation in therapy.

COMMUNITY PSYCHOLOGY

The community psychology model, with its emphasis on creating more responsive social systems and institutions, most closely approximates the activist style and preventive objectives of Black psychology. The community psychological approach differs from the traditional clinical model in the sense that the community psychologist does not wait for the individual patient to walk in for treatment (Zax and Specter, 1974). The community psychologist reaches out to the community, or "service catchment area" as it is called, with a coordinated package of preventive mental health services designed to improve the psychological well-being of people throughout the life cycle.

A typical community psychology program operating out of community mental health centers in a Black neighborhood, such as Westside in San Francisco and The Bobby E. Wright Center in Chicago, is likely to be involved in preschool activities for young children, parent development, couples workshops, tutoring for school-age children, cultural awareness training for teachers, continuing education for mental health professionals, pre-employment classes for adolescents and adults, substance abuse classes for the chemically dependent, and social activities for senior citizens.

At the same time the staff is engaged in monitoring and working as a liaison with educational, social service, law enforcement, and employment agencies. The community is the client and the Black community psychologist is like a social engineer who orchestrates a variety of functions involving several levels of social systems that impinge on the psychological well-being of Black folks. Through its education and consultative services, the comprehensive community mental health center is the umbrella agency that normally sponsors these outreach and liaison efforts. The comprehensive community mental health centers, funded by a combination of federal, state, and local sources, are required to offer a complete package of mental health services, which in addition to education and consultation include inpatient and outpatient treatment, partial hospitalization, and emergency services (Murrell, 1978).

For a community mental health center to be maximally effective, it is imperative that the community perspective be reflected in the design and delivery of services. Too often in the past, service models have been developed to do things for Black folks rather than with them. Ideally, a community mental health center in the Black community is a cooperative effort with mental health professionals and community people as equal partners, with community representation at every level of policy making and service delivery. Prior to the advent of the comprehensive mental health care centers in the Black community in the late 1960s, there existed and still exists an informal network of individuals, extended family groups, churches, and social organizations who have been looking out for the mental health needs of the community. Since the plantation days, these indigenous service providers and individual folk psychologists have been teaching people how to parent, settling family arguments, helping young people get started, calming people during periods of crisis, and providing information through the grapevine about what's going down, how to find a job, and how to deal with "the man's" social service agencies and the criminal justice system. They know what the community needs, have a high level of credibility based on a track record of successful performance, and possess a good knowledge of which programs are likely to work, through years of direct experience with field testing the programs.

An interdependent working relationship with these indigenous groups can provide the community mental health center in the Black community with credibility, political support, and expert counsel on program development. The professional staff can in turn provide resources and technical assistance to community groups in areas such as grant writing, funding sources, and office space. The church elders, grandmothers, curbstone psychologists, folk healers, spiritualists, tea leaf readers, psychic Madam Neptunes, and Brother Zoros who have already been operating as care givers should be incorporated into meaningful policy-making and service provider roles with the Black community mental health system, which is normally done by hiring them as paraprofessionals and community aides.

The idea of Black professionals and community mental health paraprofessionals working as equals may sound good on paper, but it is difficult to achieve in practice. Too often, a continuous source of friction has developed between the two groups regarding expertise, power, and the final authority in decision-making situations, with the end result being that the paraprofessionals are relegated to dead-end positions and lack a real voice in policy making. A comprehensive mental health center has the responsibility to avoid dead-end roles for community people by developing a process, conjointly with academic degree-granting institutions, that leads to increasing levels of certification, expertise, and financial remuneration through a combination of experience-based credits, in-service training, and job-related competency exams. Increasing the expertise and employability of community people through an experience-based competency and training approach was the original career ladder concept put forth in the Great Society's New Careers for the Poor (Pearl and Riessman, 1965). New careers for Black poor folks proved to be more a myth than a reality. Certification boards, professional organizations, and degree-granting institutions were reluctant to create more flexible pathways into the world of advanced degrees required for licensure as a mental health professional.

There is a vast amount of undeveloped talent in the Black community, particularly among the youth, who could increase their range of options by being trained for careers in the expanding spectrum of mental health and health-related fields, not only as practitioners but as administrators, researchers, health planners, teachers, and systems managers. A community mental health system has the opportunity to provide Black youth with direct exposure to prospective careers, role models, and informational networks in mental health and related fields through part-time jobs as peer counselors, case worker aides, research assistants, admission clerks, and general office workers. Black youth need this direct exposure to concrete experiences, combined with Black role models, of how career fields operate because they seldom have the opportunity to acquire first-hand preprofessional training in the course of their daily lives. There is also a critical shortage of fully licensed Black mental health professionals who know the Black community from the experiential perspective of having grown up in it. Early exposure of inner-city youth to mental health careers can serve as a long-range recruiting mechanism to decrease the shortage of mental health professionals who have a mixture of formal training and direct experience gained by living in the community.

The dimensions of training for community mental health systems extend beyond inner-city youth and community people. Graduate and preprofessional students, their teachers, and established mental health practitioners—Black and non-Black—can increase their understanding of the issues involved in preventive services, diagnoses, and treatment, as well as those in the administration of the overall delivery system by participating in field experiences, internships, practicums, seminars, and continuing education workshops sponsored by Black-oriented community mental health centers. The educational outreach necessary to increase the awareness of current and future professionals about Black-related mental health issues can be expanded by training affiliations between teaching institutions and community health centers that allow for the interchange of staff in teaching roles, clinical supervision, and consultation. While our descriptions of community mental health centers are rather positive and idealistic, we are mindful that too many community centers around the U.S. are ill-equipped to respond to the challenges of providing quality mental health services to the Black community. Many centers that purport to serve African-American people have no Afro-centric orientation toward service delivery. There are few, if any, African-American psychologists on staff, and no policy makers who understand the full range of issues that must be addressed in working with client populations who are African-American.

The job of improving the quality of mental health services in the Black community cannot be accomplished in isolation from the spheres of influence in the community at large. The Black mental health center is in a position to provide leadership in creating a more sophisticated consciousness of the issues by facilitating communication between the major spheres of influence, as represented by community people, youth, students in preparation for mental health careers, established minority and nonminority professionals (especially African-American psychologists), social activists, and the political power brokers.

RECOMMENDATIONS FOR SERVICE DELIVERY

White (1984) suggests that, to increase effectiveness with Black clients, both Black and non-Black therapists need to be cognizant of four major issues:

1. The impact of oppression on the lives of Blacks.
2. Afro-American psychological perspectives as a source of strength.
3. Afro-American language styles (to facilitate communication).
4. Identity concerns that arise as a result of an admixture of Afro-American and Euro-American influences.

Therapists who plan to work with African-American clients would do well to familiarize themselves with these issues.

Cultural confirmation for White's (1984) suggestions can be found in the writings of other Black psychologists. Block (1980), for example, also talks about therapist errors and cautions service providers about being influenced by, and promoting the illusion of, color blindness (e.g., "I don't view you as an African-American client, I see you as a human being"). While the intention of this statement may be admirable, such attitudes implicitly deny the authenticity of one's African makeup, and work against the client's moving toward rediscovering and maintaining Afro-centric values into their own life space.

Our observations of Black people lead us to believe that throughout one's life, African-American people will be confronted again and again with the developmental issues of becoming comfortable with one's identity, physical makeup, and ego ideal. These phenomena (issues) are similar to those articulated by Peck (1955) in his discussion of developmental crises of the late adulthood era. His research suggests that individuals in this society must successfully work through issues of identity, body image, and ego, in order to gain a sense of self-satisfaction about their lives.

Counseling and other psychological service providers need to recognize that, as long as Black people are subjected to racist and oppressive conditions in this society and are confronted with the question of how much to compromise one's "Blackness" in order to successfully assimilate, they will continue to need therapeutic assistance in struggling with issues of:

1. *Self-differentiation versus preoccupation with assimilation,* where an individual strives to become comfortable with the recognition that he/she is a worthwhile human being regardless of valuation and validation from Whites.

2. *Body transcendence versus preoccupations with body image,* where an individual strives to become comfortable with one's physical self, which may be characterized by a continuum of possibilities ranging from African to Afro-European characteristics (i.e., very dark or very light skin, very coarse or very straight hair, very thick or very thin lips).

3. *Ego transcendence versus self-absorption,* where a person strives to become secure enough in oneself to be able to develop personal ego strength by contributing to the uplifting of one's people, rather than oneself exclusively. Such efforts are consistent with the African world view of "I am because we are, and because we are, therefore, I am" (Nobles, 1972, Mbiti, 1970).

In addition to the need for a culturally specific therapeutic knowledge base, psychological service providers in particular, and service delivery agencies in general, need to struggle with the question of how to assist African-American clients in developing a commitment to remain in therapy until their presenting problems are resolved. Earlier in this chapter, we reported that better than 50 percent of ethnic clients terminate therapy after the initial session (Heitler, 1976; Sue, 1978), yet few service providers have a clue about how to eradicate this dilemma. Unlike their practicing colleagues, however, Fiester and Rudestam (1975) have recognized that lower socioeconomic class patients contributed disproportionately to the dropout rate, with unmet expectations most often being reported as reasons for their dissatisfaction. Differential expectations of clients toward therapists lead clients to expect direct authoritative opinions from therapists while they sit passively waiting to be cured. Therapists, on the other hand, often expect their clients to be more active and disclosive, and assume a greater sense of responsibility for their concerns, while they practiced a nondirective approach to assessing clients problems. When the expectations of both therapy participants are not met, clients discontinue treatment believing the therapist, or the process of therapy, to be ineffective and irrelevant, while the therapist is left with images of an uncommitted or even resistant client.

We believe that one approach that might assist service providers in facilitating client commitment to treatment is pretherapy education. This procedure involves giving clients an orientation to therapy prior to their initial session. While various mediums (audiotape, printed handouts, etc.) have been utilized, the strongest research support has been demonstrated using videotape (Dyke, 1983). Surprisingly, many mental health service delivery units have not adopted pretherapy education in any form, but we believe that this approach has merit and deserves to be tested further to empirically assess its utility.

The third recommendation centers around the recognition that therapeutic strategies promoting Afro-centric values are more likely to be effective with an African-American client who also subscribes to that value system. For example, group rather than individual psychotherapy, in some cases, may be a preferred or even more effective mode of treatment for Black clients (Shipp, 1983). While the notion of using groups is not a new idea (Brayboy, 1971; Yalom, 1975), Shipp contends that clinicians fail to recognize how and why group approaches may be effective with their Black clients. Group approaches help to promote the Afro-centric notion of collective survival, commonality among individuals, mutual cooperation, and shared responsibility, which are traditional values in the Black community. Group approaches also encourage sharing among individual members and facilitate the development of group cohesiveness. Shipp (1983) believes that studies implying that the cohesiveness from sharing experiences and backgrounds have therapeutic value often overlook the relationship between group work and the client's cultural dispositions.

Family systems approaches may also be effective modes of treatment because of the reliance on the group. Hines and Boyd-Franklin (1982), for example, document how the utilization of family kinship networks and bonds during the course of therapy with an African-American client provides an important source of support. McAdoo (1981) also suggests that reliance on natural support systems (extended family) rather than institutional supports may reduce feelings of guilt, defeat, humiliation, and powerlessness some clients feel.

A further recommendation for service providers interested in effectively treating Black clients is to familiarize themselves with a broad-based curriculum of Afro-American and African psychological principles. Nobles (1986) contends that much of what is meaningful in African psychology has gone unnoticed or unrecognized because of the inability of psychologists and other service providers to understand basic African psychological principles, which were revealed to humanity by the ancient Africans through the use of symbolism. If Nobles' contention is accurate (and we suspect it is), it seems possible that suggestions for useful treatment strategies with African-American clients may also become more crystallized if practitioners attempt to understand the symbolism of ancient African teachings.

Nobles (1986) teaches us that in ancient Africa, for example, the symbol of an animal was worshipped as an act of consecration to the vital functions characterizing the animal. "So-called primitive animal worship is not in reality the worship of animals, but a method used to identify and clarify the essential function or law of nature embodied in the particular animal" (p. 34). The jackal, for example, in ancient African thought was the symbol of judgment and represented the law of digestion. Digestion, in turn, should be viewed as a precise act of innate discrimination and analysis, wherein things ingested into the body, mind, and spirit are transformed into useful energy and separated from that which is to be discarded as waste. In essence, digestion is a destructive-productive process of transformation wherein that which contributes to the survival of the organism is stored by the body and used; that which has no usefulness to the organism's survival is expelled.

Nobles' interpretation of that law of nature through his understanding of symbolism may have some contemporary relevance for clinicians who work with African-American clients. Oppression, discrimination, and racism are unnatural human phenomena. As such, these conditions are often internalized (ingested) and help to stimulate feelings of confusion, anxiety, anger, guilt, frustration, and self-doubt in Black and African-American people. Sometimes, these factors cause them to become disconnected from self as well as from other African-Americans in spirit and in physical proximity. However, the traditional Afro-centric view of self is contingent upon the existence of an interconnectedness with other Black people. As such, therapists might need to assist clients in reconnecting themselves in body and spirit to other African-American people or at least help them to realize that their personal sense of discomfort (anxiety, guilt, confusion, etc.) may be related to being disconnected from those Black experiences.

It might even be necessary for therapists to assist Black and African-American clients in having a culturally corrective experience whereby clients are assisted in:

1. Promoting thoughts, feelings and behaviors that affirm their humanity as Black persons of African descent.
2. Purging from their mind, body, and spirit those ideas, feelings, and behaviors that prove destructive to them as organisms and do nothing to affirm their humanity as African-Americans.

Assisting an African-American client with a culturally corrective experience may also force therapists to question their role within the therapy process itself. Some theoretical orientations assume that the most important role of the clinician working with the client is to be an objective outsider who supports clients in working through their issues in ways only important to the clients.

Counseling is assumed to be an interactive process in which the therapist attempts to facilitate the client's personal awareness and movement toward self-actualization. Seldom are therapists expected to align themselves with the client or confront the client in ways that might violate the unwritten rule of remaining neutral, anonymous, objective, passive listeners or observers. However, Basch (1980) reminds us that there is nothing wrong with influencing the client, and there is no ideal way for therapists to behave. Certainly, non-psychodynamically oriented theories practice alternate approaches.

Indeed, we would contend that a theoretical orientation that encourages therapists to be subjective companions rather than just objective outsiders may be an effective approach with African-American clients. Therapists adopting a subjective companion role attempt to become interpersonally connected to the client (development of a kinship bond), and may be guided by personal biases about what is ultimately best for the client's mental health. The therapist's attitudes are influenced by the recognition that confronting clients about their self-destructive attitudes and beliefs may be the catalyst that stimulates a client's movement towards becoming a self-actualizing Black/African-American. Therapists should be cautious, however, about interpreting the client's self-actualization efforts as a process of simply becoming a better individual for self's sake. In the African ethos (Nobles, 1972, 1980, 1986; Mbiti, 1970), the self one seeks to become is related to and influenced by a more collective consciousness defined by the community or group. Unlike Western philosophical systems, the African tradition does not place heavy emphasis on the individual; it is recognized that only in terms of other people does one become conscious of his or her own being. Only through others does one learn the responsibilities toward him/herself and others (Nobles, 1980, p. 29).

THE INFLUENCE OF IDENTITY STATES ON THE THERAPEUTIC RELATIONSHIP

Regardless of which theoretical orientation a psychologist chooses to adopt, one factor seems to remain constant. That is, the relationship between the therapist and the client is a vital and necessary part of the therapeutic process (Highlen & Hill, 1984).

Parham (1981, 1989) has recommended that service providers look beyond the client's skin color or racial self-designation (i.e., Black, Negro, African-American, etc.) in trying to determine an appropriate therapeutic match. Furthermore, he asserts that recognizing the within-group variability among African-American clients may assist a therapist in understanding how the racial identity attitudes of a client discussed in Chapter 3 may influence the ability to establish a qualitative (workable) relationship with that client (Parham, 1989). Figure 6.2 provides an illustration of how racial identity attitudes impact the ability of service providers to break down the social distance between themselves and the client.

For example, Caucasian therapists who begin treatment with a Black person possessing pro-White/anti-Black attitudes will have little difficulty breaking down the social distance between themselves and the client, where ethnicity is concerned. However, one might expect ethnicity to be an obstacle if the client treated by Caucasian therapists were more immersed in his or her racial identity.

Given this latter scenario, readers should be cautioned against inferring that a relationship between White therapists and Black clients with strong ethnic identification is impossible. Indeed, positive therapeutic work can occur if the issues related to the client's perception of the therapist are worked through in the initial stages of therapy.

Service providers should also be cautious about assuming that an inability of the client to become "hooked" on the therapy process is indicative of client resistance and/or of factors beyond therapists' control. While this may be the case in some instances, it is also possible that the service provider has not spent sufficient time exploring trust issues related to cross-ethnic interactions and relationships.

Figure 6.2 also provides a prediction of the ability of a Black therapist to work with Black clients at various attitudinal stages. This issue is particularly important since many service providers and even entire agencies assume that a Black staff member is a better therapeutic match for Black clients in every case. Such a practice would be questionable if a Black therapist were matched with a client with strong pre-encoun-

FIGURE 6.2.

STAGE	BLACK/WHITE ATTITUDES	WHITE COUNSELOR/BLACK CLIENT	SOCIAL DISTANCE	BLACK COUNSELOR/BLACK CLIENT
Pre-encounter	Pro-White Anti-Black		Ability to establish trust, rapport, etc.	
Encounter	Confusion-Black Confusion-White			
Immersion- Emmersion	Pro-Black Anti-White			
Internalization	Pro-Black (Accepting White)			

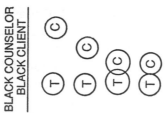

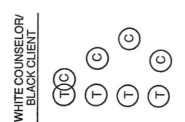

Parham (1989).

ter attitudes. One consequence of such an interaction might be premature termination by clients who believe that the therapist is an "Affirmative Action Psychologist" who is less qualified than a White counterpart and thus less capable of delivering effective treatment.

In the same context, it is also inappropriate to assume that ethnicity alone and not training is a necessary and sufficient criterion to work with a client. This assumption is also questionable since most Black service providers receive similar training and degrees as their White counterparts, with little if any ethnic content as part of their core curriculum. Arguably, similarity in ethnic background may provide one with a common life experience, but such is not always the case. Certainly, courses in African-American psychology are essential, and are considered by us to be a minimum prerequisite for anyone working with Black clients.

CHAPTER SEVEN

CONTEMPORARY ISSUES CONFRONTING THE BLACK COMMUNITY

Growing up in the Black community allows most Black people to be exposed to the full spectrum of experiences that life has to offer. Inevitably, if they live long enough, Black men and women will be touched by experiences that bring pain and pleasure, sorrow and joy, tragedy and resilience, and even loneliness and love. They also see death, chronic illness, poverty, homicides, the debilitating effects of drugs and alcohol, crime, and the lives of Black men and women filled with apathy, despair, and hopelessness. While it is difficult to predict which experiences one will inevitably encounter at a given moment, the one predictable element in life is time. Despite generational differences between this book's coauthors, for example, we were indoctrinated with similar perspectives on time. In the Black community, there is one saying that goes, "One thing is for certain and the rest is lies, and that's that time flies."[1]

Clearly, time is marching on. As we flow with the tides ushering the 1980s out and the 1990s in, it is important for African-American people to take a good look at the issues that confront the Black community today and the challenges that we all must face tomorrow. We have selected three issues with contemporary relevance that represent significant challenges for the future: male-female relationships, the endangered Black male, and the need for our youth to develop social competency skills. Our intention is merely to lay the issues out in a clear, identifiable fashion; no attempt will be made to achieve resolution. The ultimate solution must come from the Black community and the larger American society.

MALE-FEMALE RELATIONSHIPS

In the first edition of *The Psychology of Blacks*, White (1984) discusses the status of male-female relations. He suggested that the ideal relationship between Black males and females is one characterized by the values of interdependence, cooperation, mutual respect, and an absence of rigid sex-role distinctions regarding economics, household responsibilities, and social roles. According to White, "relationships that are built on a bond of sharing, nurturance, tenderness, and appreciation have the strong psychological foundation necessary to cope with the social and economic stresses that usually confront Black couples living in a country dominated by Euro-American values" (p. 73). This second edition aims to support those propositions.

White also recognized a tension between Black males and females, which prevented them from achieving the satisfaction in relationships each so desperately desired. In the years since that first edition was published, much has changed and nothing has changed. Many Black females and males have begun to talk with rather than about each other, and are making attempts to understand and respect their mutual interests and individual differences. Undoubtedly, those who have been successful at bridging the communication gap are finding that their relationships are more satisfying and mutually supportive.

Others, however, have not found the keys that unlock the door to this kind of relationship. Some can identify potential mates and initiate a relationship, but have difficulty maintaining longevity. Some receive sufficient attention from the opposite sex only to find that it is not from the "right person." Still others are convinced that due to the shortage of potential mates, or previous experiences that had a negative or unpleasant outcome, the chances of their developing a solid relationship or even finding companionship are "slim and none." Indeed, pessimism is in the air. The quest for a suitable mate has led both males and females to extend the parameters of what are appropriate choices regarding life style, ages of mates, and sexual preferences. In fact, if one peruses selected articles written in magazines popular in the Black community (i.e., *Essence* or *Ebony*), one can clearly see both genders struggling with these issues. The shortage of men has led many women to confront the issues of achieving happiness and satisfaction being single (Harayda, 1987). Males, and especially females, are changing ideas about the "right age" of one's mate, as many women are becoming more comfortable with younger mates and younger men are becoming more comfortable with older women (Moore-Campbell, 1987). Couples, both married and unmarried, are changing ideas about residing in the same geographic location as many men and women are committing to relationships while maintaining separate residences in different cities and even on different coasts (Ray, 1989).

The resolve of some females and males to struggle with personal and logistical challenges to maintaining relationships in the eighties and nineties is a promising sign. For other members of the Black community, however, no such promise is forthcoming. If one listens to the rhythm and blues music of today, it is clear that both males and females are having tremendous difficulty connecting to each other. Songs with lyrics such as "got to have a J-O-B if you want to be with me," "ain't nothing going on but the rent"[2], and "thanks for my child"[3] speak about the feelings of pain, distrust, and irresponsibility both males and females harbor towards each other.

Indeed, we have observed that, like flowers struggling to bloom, Black male-female relationships are finding their roots to new growth being strangled by the weeds of selfishness, exploitation, deceit, faulty expectations, self-centeredness, poor timing, and sometimes bad luck. We also recognize, however, that the first step toward analyzing the problems between males and females, and ultimately toward resolving the conflicts, is to accurately identify the conflict. Rather than participate in name calling and finger pointing, we have chosen to merely identify the issues that we believe are salient to male-female relationships. It is our hope that, once these issues are identified, both males and females will use them as a basis for dialogue and honest exchange.

The four issues are trust, sex and sexuality, control, and social roles.

TRUST

Trust is defined as "confidence in the ability or intention of a person" (*Random House Dictionary*, 1967). Trust in the Black community is knowing where people are "coming from" and believing they are for real. Trust issues, or the lack thereof, manifest themselves through the inhibited risk-taking styles often practiced by both males and females as each waits for the other to sufficiently demonstrate some level of commitment to a relationship (or potential relationship) before investing any amount of time, money, feelings, and ego. Who calls whom first and how often, who pays first and what amount, who initially finds whom attractive and how much, and who says "I love you" first are all issues frequently questioned.

While such questions inevitably serve to defend our male and female egos against a possible fear of rejection, they also insert arbitrary hurdles and unnecessary games into the relationship and stifle their growth. Both males and females must ask themselves why these issues are important, and each must confront his or her own fears and personal insecurities regarding the relationship.

The real question is not whether we can trust the other person. Such a question seeks to externalize one's responsibility for feelings that rightly belong to each of us. Rather, the ultimate question is, "can each of us, as a male or female, trust ourselves enough to take a risk on someone else?"

In our observations of Black male-female relationships, we have also observed a willingness on the part of both men and women in the initial stages of their relationship to inconvenience ourselves in order to make their partners happy and hopefully receive their validation. Going out of their way seems trivial if their efforts succeed in satisfying their partner's needs. In essence, an individual's own needs become secondary to the needs of the other person, and one partner begins to trust that the other will meet his or her own needs.

There comes a time, however, once the relationship is on solid ground and both parties feel secure, when the focus of the relationship shifts from being "other-centered" to "self-centered." Both males and females begin to see their own needs as primary and the needs of their partner as secondary. Whether unconscious or conscious, intentional or not, such practices often leave one or both persons in the relationship feeling neglected, used, and unimportant. Another question or issue Black males and females need to discuss is how they can rediscover or develop the trust that allowed them to put the other's needs first, while trusting that their needs will also be met.

SEX AND SEXUALITY

Issues related to sex and sexuality are among the most frequently discussed topics between Black males and females. Questions that are frequently raised include:

At what age is it appropriate to become sexually active?
At what point in the relationship are sexual relations appropriate—first date, third date, once married?
If we become sexually involved, is our relationship exclusive?
Is our sexual involvement indicative of any special feelings for one another?

The answers to these questions will undoubtedly be influenced by variables such as personal upbringing, values, religious orientation, previous experiences, and one's feelings at a given moment.

Further observation of Black males and females shows that they appear to have difficulty both in expressing their opinions on these issues comfortably and in understanding the opinions of their gender counterparts. Assuming sex and sexuality remain an integral part of relationships, each must attempt to understand what the other is thinking and feeling.

Questions of teenage sexuality raise a number of controversial issues. Most responsible adults are against teenage sex. We believe that sex among teenagers is contraindicated until young people have matured to the point that they can seriously, responsibly, and honestly discuss with their partner issues of safe sex, birth control, and long-term commitment in the relationship.

Our belief is that sexual activity among children and young teens should be discouraged, especially when they are unable to appreciate and fully comprehend the responsibilities of safe sex and the consequences of teenage pregnancy. Consequently, adult role models in the Black community will need to assist youth in exploring their natural sexual curiosity in an educational context, and teaching them how to control their physical and mental attractions.

When two consenting adults are engaged in a relationship and physical intimacy is a component of that relationship, each will need to help the other deal with several issues. The first is safe sex and the responsibility associated with physical intimacy in a relationship. In an age when AIDS and unplanned pregnancy are both escalating, these issues should be thoroughly discussed.

The question of when it is appropriate to explore a sexual component in a relationship is a complex one. Black females need males to understand that sexual involvement often requires a commitment to "be there" after the moments of intimacy have passed. Regardless of whether sexual intimacy is achieved after the first, third, or tenth date, the expectation of commitment is likely to be there for most women.

Black men and women will also need to work through issues of relationship definition, parameters, and expectations, particularly as they relate to exclusivity. For example, if a male respects a woman's decision to abstain from sexual intimacy, and applies no pressure on her to force the issue, is he then obligated to abstain himself, or is it appropriate for him to seek sexual satisfaction elsewhere? How would this affect their relationship?

Issues of attractiveness are another area of concern. Black men and women need to discuss issues centered around feelings of attraction for one another and the need to act on them. Women, and especially men, learn through socialization how they should respond in a given moment when faced with being attracted to someone. Usually, males and females alike begin to ponder the possibilities and potentialities for such an interaction, and, unfortunately, avenues for exploring a potential friendship are too often abandoned in favor of those that reduce the interaction to an assessment of a potential for sexual conquest. How can Black men and women relate to each other as friends?

A final topic worth mentioning regarding Black male-female sexuality is the need to develop more direct ways of communicating thoughts, feelings, and intentions to each other without using sex as a vehicle or a crutch. While physical intimacy can be a direct expression of deep affection and love for another person, it is often used as a distraction that only inhibits both men and women from direct verbal communication with each other. Physical intimacy can also leave one or the other party confused as to the real intentions of the other, and what specifically the act of lovemaking represents to that relationship.

CONTROL

Control is defined "as power or authority to guide or manage" (*Webster's*, 1986). With respect to male-female relationships, control refers to the need or desire on the part of one or both parties to influence, direct, and even dictate the course of the relationship and/or the behavior of the other party involved. In relationships, disagreements about managing time, money, and friends often boil down to control. Questions arise, such as:

> Who will choose the friends and how do we incorporate them into the relationship?
> Whose interests (job, hobbies) are more important?
> Who will determine the pace and direction of the relationship?

These questions, as well as who acquiesces to whom, are all manifestations of control issues. Both males and females exercise various amounts of control in an attempt to meet their needs in the relationship. At a deeper level, control issues are related to trust issues, in that one's willingness to relinquish control in a relationship depends on one's ability to trust the other party with providing for his or her needs.

INSTRUMENTAL VERSUS EXPRESSIVE ROLES

Within the context of normal relationships, males and females are likely to adopt (through either choice or socialization) certain roles when relating to one another. Not surprisingly, the roles adopted by each will likely conform to roles that are perceived to be gender-appropriate. Socialized to be the leaders, the major decision makers, and primary wage earners, males perceive themselves as the instrumental role players. Females, on the other hand, are often expected to yield to male assertions of authority, be responsible for providing the emotional support, take primary responsibility for rearing the children and managing the household; they adopt the more expressive roles. In some cases, these traditional role assignments prove very functional for Black couples.

In other cases, Black males and females have considerable difficulty in adopting these more traditional roles. In addition to the fact that these roles are often based on rigid, Euro-centric sex-role distinctions, the major difficulty with these role assignments is that they do not reflect contemporary life style choices and realities for Black males and females.

Both Black men and women are encouraged to explore job and career opportunities in adulthood. Since many young people are choosing to delay marriage until a career is well underway (regardless of whether they have already borne children or not), both men and women will bring similar assets and needs into the relationship. Both will likely be independent; each may have a job; both parties will either live alone, with a roommate, or at home; and each will have the needs for love, companionship, nurturance, friendship, respect, cooperation, admiration, and support. Problems usually result when either party is expected to conform to a social role (norm) that they have not explicitly endorsed. For example, when a woman proves to be an effective independent decision maker, earns as much or more of a salary as her partner, and wants to be recognized as equal in the relationship, the male may have difficulty adjusting. Similarly, if a man is expected to carry the responsibility for financially supporting the relationship (through periods of dating and courtship, living together, and/or marriage), despite the fact that both people work, he may feel burdened. Also, since males are typically expected to initiate relationships, and risk rejection while waiting for confirmation from the female on everything from phone numbers to future dates, he may now expect females to participate in the initiation phases of the relationship and be more assertive while becoming less assertive himself.

Black males and females must understand that role expectations of each other are changing; consequently, each needs to provide greater levels of empathy and sensitivity to each other. Females expect to participate with males in shared decision making, expect males to become more active in child rearing, and look for greater levels of emotional intimacy and support from their mates. Conversely, males may need assistance in shouldering the financial responsibilities of a relationship, and adjusting their self-images as men to incorporate more expressive roles.

Ultimately, Black males and females in particular (and Black families in general) will need to better discuss and communicate about two primary questions:

Who is responsible for financially supporting a family and making the major decisions?
Who is responsible for rearing the children?

The latter question speaks not only to masculine/feminine roles, but also to the role of Black families, versus that of the federal government and the welfare system, in providing for the needs of its members.

For Black males and females to have a better chance at positive, productive relationships, they must first seek a deeper level of understanding from each other, and know what the other thinks and feels. Agreement is ideal, but not an absolute necessity. Rather, empathy requires an understanding of feelings and opinions, in respecting such feelings and opinions as their own.

THE ENDANGERED BLACK MALE

The fact that Black men are rapidly becoming an endangered species is a phenomenon being discussed in many circles. Some authors have argued, with good reason, that social forces, as well as environmental and institutional factors, contribute to Black men becoming a population at risk (Johnson, 1983; Gibbs, 1988). These factors include:

Over-representation of Black males in prisons (42 percent of inmate population).

Discriminatory judicial practices and a lack of adequate legal representation.

Poor education.

Unemployment (28 to 30 percent among Black men, up to 48 percent among Black youth).

Inadequate health care.

In the last two decades, much of the energy generated in confronting these negative elements in American society is directed at systemic factors (i.e., creating job programs, hiring more Black police officers, appointing more Black judges, and creating educational programs). Yet Parham (1987) reminds us that by restricting interventions to external forces alone, public policies and social commentaries have implied that Black men have no part in alleviating their predicament as a population at risk, and that they lack the mental fortitude to deal effectively with adverse conditions in society. Parham believes such conclusions are questionable, given that Black men have survived and persevered through hundreds of years of oppression in the United States. We agree, in fact, that African-American men must simultaneously shoulder some of the blame for their predicament and some of the responsibility for developing personal intervention strategies that will ultimately better their condition.

Parham's (1987) analysis is particularly penetrating when one considers that not only do African-American males have the shortest life expectancy average when compared to other U.S. citizens, but they also appear to be coconspirators in their destruction. Staples (1982) reported that the overall homicide rate for Black men is significantly higher than that of any age group: 42 percent of all homicide victims are Black, and the majority of the perpetrators of these crimes are also Black, predominantly male, and usually under 24 years of age.

Black youth have a 50 percent higher probability of dying before the age of twenty than their White counterparts (U.S. Department of Health, Education and Welfare, 1978). Comparison data will also show that, for Black youth, homicide, drug abuse, suicide, and accidents are the leading killers, whereas accidents and cardiovascular disease are the primary culprits for White youth (Staples, 1982). There have been various attempts in the literature to explain this increase in homicides among Blacks (Poussaint, 1972; Staples, 1982), with explanations ranging from psychological to sociological variables. Regardless of what explanation one adopts, however, the bottom line is still the same—Black people are killing Black people. Certainly, the rising tide of gang violence plaguing the inner cities of this nation is a case in point.

In extending his analysis, Parham (1987) also notes that another factor affecting the average life expectancy of Black men is physical illness. That many members of the Black community, especially men, are subjected to inadequate health care (either through lack of facilities or because of underuse) has long been recognized as a contributing factor to the short life expectancy of Black men. The consequences of this dilemma, however, are becoming increasingly dramatic. Proportionally, Black men now have higher rates of cancer than do any other group in the United States, and today the disease is killing twice as many Black men as it did thirty years ago (Johnson, 1983). Reports also indicate that although Black men are affected with various forms of cancer (e.g., prostate, colon-rectum, stomach), the most prevalent is lung cancer. Although nutritional, life style, and other environmental factors are often implicated, the most substantial contributor seems to be cigarette smoking (Johnson, 1983). In fact, Johnson (1983) reported findings of the American Cancer Society indicating that Black men smoke more cigarettes than do those in all other age-sex groups in America. Ironically, lung cancer is one of the most difficult forms of cancer to cure and the easiest to prevent.

Another factor that has long been recognized for its impact on the physical and mental health of Black men is alcohol abuse. In fact, Bourne (1973) rated alcoholism as one of the leading mental health problems facing the Black community. Bourne's findings are now shared by the National Institute of Mental Health who rate chemical dependency and substance abuse as the number one mental health problem in America. The consequences of alcohol abuse, which negatively affect both the personal and social lives of Black men, include substantial increases in rates of homicide, arrests, accidents, assualts, and physical illness (Harper, 1981). Harper (1981), however, suggested that the major barrier to treatment for Black men is a refusal to accept the concept of alcoholism.

For many Black men, heavy drinking is the norm and is perceived as an attribute of manhood and camaraderie. Because they do not draw a clear line between use and abuse, many Black men who drink excessively refuse to accept any alcohol treatment or other medical assistance (Harper, 1979; Williams, 1975). It is also important to recognize that many of the physical illnesses and problems Black men face are stress related.

Another alarming statistic of the 1980s is that the suicide rate for Black people in general and Black men in particular is escalating. Analysis of statistical patterns associated with suicide suggest that, as urban residents of lower-than-average-per-capita income, Blacks should be least likely to commit suicide (Davis, 1981). This, however, is not the case. In fact, King (1982) reported that the rate of Afro-American suicide victims in major metropolitan U.S. cities was expected to exceed the overall national average for 1980 by nearly 3.5 per 100,000. After examining the 1970s data from the U.S. Census Bureau, King (1982) also reported that suicide among Black Americans has been primarily a phenomenon among youth. Among Black men and women, the largest percentage of suicides occurs among the age group of 20–34, with a 3-to-1 ratio of men to women.

Dramatic increases in suicide rates, however, are apparent when analyzed retrospectively over the last 20–25 years. The data clearly indicate that the suicide rate for young Black men has been increasing steadily since the 1960s (Davis, 1981). The sharp increase in the suicide rate of young Blacks lends credibility to the notion that their lives are characterized by higher levels of stress. Ironically, much of the stress, tension, and even hostility that Black men must endure originates from sources intended to support them. Nowhere is this dilemma more accurately illustrated than in the educational system.

Patton (1981) argued that, as the primary socializing agent, elementary and secondary education has negatively affected the achievements, self-concepts, and selected dispositional aspects of Black men. The cumulative gap between Blacks and Whites in educational achievement levels begins with kindergarten and increases through the post-secondary years (Williams, 1974). Additional indications of the negative consequences that the educational system has on Black men lie in the suspension rates, dropout-pushout rates, and subsequent college attendance rates of Black men. Cottle (1975) noted that Black children are suspended three times as frequently as their White peers and for longer periods. These data, along with research suggesting that Black male students are disproportionately tracked into slower classes and lack adequate role models throughout their time in the educational system (Patton, 1981), helped to clarify why Black male students are among the lowest groups in college eligibility and attendance rates (Thomas, 1977).

From the evidence cited in this brief review, it is clear that Black men are facing times of extreme hardship. Furthermore, this trend is likely to continue for the foreseeable future. As such, the marshaling of societal change agents and the modification of personal behaviors are mandates that can no longer be ignored.

DEVELOPING SOCIAL COMPETENCIES

In the first edition of *The Psychology of Blacks*, White (1984) was clear in his observations that, long before children can verbalize, they are aware of the fact that something is fundamentally wrong in the American society, that some pervasive, catastrophic, and oppressive force is preventing African-American people from achieving their goals and participating in the range of opportunities provided by America for its citizens (Baldwin, 1963). The complete impact of this awareness does not come all at once, according to White, but falls into place gradually during middle childhood, preadolescence, and early adolescence. As children look into the mirror image of society reflected in television, movies, newspapers, and stories about heros of American history, they see White Americans projected with an imagery of power, courage, competence, beauty, and goodness. Listening to parents and other adults within the extended family networks, they hear about how Black people have little control over jobs, the price of food, rent levels, wages, lengthened jail sentences, and other social conditions.

The conclusion that racism is pervasive in the American society has a profound and lasting influence on African-American people. They may express their disappointment with anger, fear, resentment, or bitterness. The conclusions cannot help but generate a period of confusion in Black youth, because it forces them to deal with contradictions that have been inherent in American society for over 350 years. On the one hand, children hear that this is the land of equal opportunity, liberty, and justice for all, and that all human beings are created equal and endowed by their Creator with certain inalienable rights. Yet the reality of experience has made children aware of the fact that this is definately not the case for them.

Our observations of life in the Black community all across America lead us to a disturbing conclusion: Black people in general and Black youth in particular, are losing their ability to successfully negotiate their way through life in ways that lead to positive outcomes and the development of a full range of choices and options. The perseverance, mutual support, cooperation, and determination of our ancestors stand in sharp contrast to the values and attitudes of today's young generation. Our youth seem to have been overwhelmed by oppressive conditions to the point that they feel powerless to change, affect, and/or influence their present conditions. They

They are so focused on day-to-day survival in their immediate communities, that they often ignore the necessity of developing skills required to compete in the larger society. Our children are required to cope with pressures from gangs, lunch money shakedowns, extortion, and getting to and from school in deteriorating neighborhoods plagued by high incidences of homicide, assault, armed robbery, alcoholism, and drug activity.

But what are we to do? In addition to the formal curriculum taught in the classrooms of our educational institutions throughout this country, our children have a need to learn social competency skills. Essentially, social competency skills are the attitudes and behaviors that allow a youngster to confront the day-to-day hardships of living and emerge from those confrontations with a successful range of choices that lead to a positive outcome. Such skills and knowledges might include a repertoire of interpersonal skills:

Assertiveness training: Techniques or skills that allow individuals to communicate their thoughts, feelings, and intentions to others effectively, and in some cases receive such feedback from others more comfortably.

Communication skills: Skills that allow persons to articulate verbal and nonverbal messages in clear, concise, and understandable language.

Conflict resolution skills: Skills allowing different parties to meet their own needs (in nonaggressive, nonhostile ways) when their desires, needs, and wishes are incompatible with each other.

Ideas of self-determination: When individuals come to realize that they have personal control and power over their lives and use such power to maintain and enhance the individual and collective self.

Knowledge of career pathways: When individuals are taught how to engage in a step-by-step sequential process designed to move them from their present circumstance to a career objective, while acquiring the necessary prerequisites along the way.

Job search skills: Skills that allow a person to develop a job objective, research a company, develop a resume, apply for a job, prepare for an interview, negotiate a salary, and accept a position.

Cooperative economics: Knowledge and skills necessary to make individuals' purchasing power benefit themselves and their community.

Other valuable skills and knowledges include values clarification, interpersonal communication skills, the ability to develop support systems, the use of nonchemical highs, and stress reduction.

If we can be successful in teaching these skills to our youth, perhaps they will be less vulnerable to developing self-destructive behaviors as ways of coping with life's adversities.

CHALLENGES FOR THE BLACK COMMUNITY IN THE 1990S

Some readers may be tempted to take our observations as an indictment against African-American people and the Black community. Such a scenario would be unfortunate indeed. Our intention in sharing these observations is to challenge African-American people, the Black community, and those who work with African-Americans to help create avenues whereby Black people can better help themselves. Despite the fact that racism is alive and well, we are suggesting that, for Black people to have any chance at opportunity, they need to be taught a wide range of relationship skills, social competency skills, and attitudes of self-determination at early ages. Such skills will ultimately provide us with the fortification necessary to negotiate our way through life's inevitable obstacles.

The first strategy in fortifying ourselves is to harness the best of what the Black community has to offer. In essence, Black psychologists must find a way to capture the spirit of the culture and help that spirit to penetrate through the cognitions, emotions, and behaviors of Black people.

African-American culture has provided much in the way of resources. Nobles (1980) provides us with a description of Afro-centric values that emphasize human vitality, openness to feelings, collective survival, mutual support, and interdependence.

In a similar way, White (1984) has identified six recurring themes found in the language, oral tradition, and expressive patterns of Black people (discussed in Chapter 2). These include:

> Emotional vitality.
> Realness.
> Resilience.
> Distrust and deception.
> Interrelatedness.
> The value of direct experience.

Karenga (1966) has also articulated seven principles of Nguzo Saba designed to reinforce and strengthen our collective self-concepts as Black people in America. These principles include:

> Umoja (unity).
> Kujichagulia (self-determination).
> Ujima (collective work and responsibility).
> Ujamaa (cooperative economics).
> Nia (purpose).
> Kuumba (creativity).
> Imani (faith).

Also, Nobles (1986) has identified several African-American styles of responding to and manipulating our reality, which have their roots in African beingness. Psychologically, the techniques associated with our cultural dispositions include:

> *Improvisation:* Where one seeks to spontaneously create, invent, or arrange a known experience, situation or event such that the known experiences are extended into the unknown, thereby resulting in new experience.

Transcendence: A quality, state, or ability to exceed, go beyond, or rise above the limits of an experience, condition, or situation.

Transformation: The predisposition to recognize that the condition, quality, or nature of an experience or element has the potential to change into a different experience or element.

These techniques, principles, recurring themes, and values provide prescriptions for African-American thoughts, feelings, and behaviors. They also serve as cultural prerequisites for the maintenance and survival of African-American people. The remaining task is to synthesize these systems in an attempt to create a cultural oneness or collective consciousness wherein people can begin to endorse and share a common psychological life space.

A retrospective look at historical and contemporary legacies leads us to conclude that it is difficult for a "collective spirit" of the people to thrive in a destructive social environment. Helping people to adjust psychologically, without the benefits of a formative environment, creates a mentally healthy individual who is vulnerable to social pathology. As such, the second key strategy is to assist members of the Black community in becoming social engineers. Social engineering requires the design, construction, use, and, if necessary, modification of social structures within the Black community such that they become instruments of healthy survival and growth. Dilapidated and inferior schools plagued with poor instruction, unmotivated teachers, inadequate resources, and behavior problems must be transformed into functional educational systems where the discovery of knowledge is the first priority. Sufficient opportunities for employment and job skill development must be created for every willing and able-bodied person. Provisions need to be made to allow every person in the community, regardless of income, to receive adequate and affordable health care. Similarly, opportunities to reside in safe, clean, affordable housing must also be created and maintained.

Undoubtedly, any attempts to be successful at social engineering will require the support, cooperation, and assistance of many determined individuals and groups. Community residents will need to work side by side with local politicians, ministers, and educators, as well as with city, state, and federal agencies. Community self-determination, coupled with social responsibility from those in power, is a necessary combination.

CHAPTER EIGHT

CONCLUSION

In the preceding chapters, we have attempted to clarify the basic psychological dimensions and recurring themes in the African-American frame of reference and to describe how this perspective is reflected in the language, family dynamics, education, mental health, and life style choices of African-American people. Our attempt to explore and clarify the complexity of the psychological experiences of Blacks in America has also stimulated our need to take a retrospective look at Black psychology as a discipline, while also exploring the issues that represent our challenges for the future.

While the study of the Black psyche may be many thousands of years old (Nobles, 1986), the contemporary, more formalized movement of Black psychology has been active for approximately twenty-one years (since 1968). During the past three decades, we have observed that Black psychology as a discipline has proceded through at least two phases. The first phase involved the context of creativity. African-American psychologists began to move away from the practice of psychological reactance, where we were constantly responding to the racist, Euro-centric paradigms promoted and supported by White psychologists. The shift in perspective helped up to focus on creating, developing, and highlighting new Afro-centrically oriented ideas, constructs, and models that served as the foundation for our line of inquiry. The elders of our discipline are primarily responsible for this foundation.

The second phase was one of confirmation, in which new generations of African-American psychologists have begun to empirically test and quantitatively assess the concepts and theories proposed by earlier generations of psychologists. One of the more promising trends to emerge during this latter phase was the development and use of our Afro-centrically oriented research definitions and paradigms. In fact, the use of the term "African-American" in more recent literature to define our discipline and our people is no accident, for it represents the continuing struggle to define ourselves and our context of study as accurately as possible. Certainly, 21-year-olds must know who they are before they can know where they are really going.

As we move forward to the 1990s, life presents us with some promising opportunities and some formidable challenges. It is our suspicion that the yardstick by which our integrity and credibility as a discipline will be measured will not be based on our ability to engage in intellectual discourse among ourselves. On the contrary, members of the Black community (those currently living, those from the past, and those yet to be born) will hold us to a higher standard than that. Despite the wealth of psychological theories, models, concepts, and constructs, African-American psychologists may be in danger of becoming a community of scholars whose only merit is to engage in intellectual discourse among ourselves and our students. Certainly, many African-American psychologists are skilled academicians, but does their academic instruction help their students translate that body of knowledge into functional formulas to teach others? Many more African-American psychologists are skilled clinicians, but do their therapeutic interventions really help their patients and clients realize their potential or help others live more mentally healthy, self-actualizing lives? The reality of our existence in America shows us that the masses of our people are not in institutions of higher learning, nor can they afford the financial expense to visit psychologists in weekly therapy sessions. If we as African-American psychologists are not successful at translating our psychological theories, constructs, and models into strategies that can be operationalized by the masses of our people, then somehow we will have failed in our responsibilities.

In our opinion, the key to phase three of the Black psychology movement is applied psychology and social engineering. As African-American psychologists, we need to apply our ideas to enhance the quality of life in the Black community. We need to utilize the ideas in Black psychology to facilitate the learning of children in schools. The development of model curricula for preschool, primary, and secondary grade youngsters, as well as the establishment of learning centers that teach our children in culturally congruent learning modes would be an excellent start. We need to utilize our knowledge to enhance and enrich the quality of relationships among and between males, females, children, and families. We need to use our psychology to assist African-American people in developing and utilizing a conscious awareness of ourselves as African people, which is a necessary prerequisite for achieving mental health. We need to use our psychology to reverse the cycle of destruction that is impacting our African-American males, and to increase the political power and ideas of self-determination of people in our communities such that they begin to control the forces and institutions impacting their lives. We need to use our knowledge and expertise to impact the psychology training programs that graduate mental health professionals who will provide services to African-American people. If we, as African-American psychologists, can successfully move our people toward empowerment, then much will have been accomplished.

Because a new phase emerges does not mean that the first and second phases end. On the contrary, African-American psychologists should continue to create, confirm, and modify ideas such that our discipline does not become lost in the pool of stagnation impeding our growth potential. In essence, we must find ways of integrating knowledge and experiences from the first twenty-one years of existence, while continuously adding new ideas. We should incorporate into short- and long-term planning goals the strategies, models, and concepts that demonstrate the greatest potential for increasing the range of options and choices for African-Americans, making our environment more responsive, and generally enhancing the quality of life for all members of the Black community.

Black psychologists must also take seriously the responsibility to become social engineers. For years, we criticized traditional psychological theories for their failure to recognize systemic factors in the assessment of the etiology of psychopathology. Consequently, many African-American clients and patients were treated with therapeutic techniques inadvertently designed to help them adjust to a social environment that was oppressive, because the theories assumed the individual rather than the environment to be responsible for a client's mental problems. It is important that African-American psychologists take their criticisms of traditional psychological approaches to heart. We must recognize that many presenting problems clients disclose may provide mental health workers with evidence of structural defects in the foundation of social policies and practices. As African-American psychologists committed to social engineering, we must continue to use client concerns as a barometer for social change.

REFERENCE NOTES

CHAPTER TWO

1. With assistance from Dr. Horace Mitchell, University of California, Irvine.

CHAPTER FOUR

1. Copyright 1926 by Alfred A. Knopf, Inc., and renewed 1954 by Langston Hughes. Reprinted from *Selected Poems of Langston Hughes*, by Langston Hughes, by permission of the publisher.
2. Appears on "I've Got to Use My Imagination" album by Gladys Knight (1973).
3. Larry Neal, "The Ethos of the Blues," *The Black Scholar* (1972), pp. 42–48. Reprinted by permission.
4. Reprinted by permission of Harold Ober Associates Incorporated. Copyright 1950 by Langston Hughes. Renewed 1978 by George H. Bass as Executor for the Estate of Langston Hughes.
5. James Baldwin, *The Fire Next Time*. Copyright 1963, 1962 by James Baldwin. Permission granted by The Dial Press and Michael Joseph Ltd.
6. Hortense Spillers, "Martin Luther King and the Style of The Black Sermon," *The Black Scholar* (September 1971), pp. 14–27. Reprinted by permission.

7. From "I Have a Dream" by Martin Luther King, Jr. Copyright 1963 by Martin Luther King, Jr. Reprinted by permission of Joan Daves.

8. Ibid.

9. Grace Holt, "Metaphor, Black Discourse Style and Cultural Reality," in R. L. Williams (ed.), *Ebonics, The True Langauge of Black Folks* (St. Louis: Institute of Black Studies, 1975), p. 87.

10. Ethnotropism is the use of a word, phrase, or utterance in a different cultural context for the purpose of giving life or emphasis to an idea (Holt, 1975).

11. H. Rap Brown, *Die Nigger Die*. Copyright 1969 by Lynn Brown. Permission granted by The Dial Press and Allison & Busby Ltd.

12. Baldwin, James, *Notes of a Native Son* (Boston: Beacon Press, 1955).

13. Appears in "Mudbone" from the album by Richard Pryor, "Is It Something I Said?" (New York: Reprise Records, 1975). Reprinted by permission.

14. From *Robert Kennedy and His Times,* by Arthur M. Schlesinger, Jr. Copyright 1978 by Arthur M. Schlesinger, Jr. Reprinted by permission of Houghton Mifflin Company.

15. D. Brown, *Bury My Heart at Wounded Knee* (New York: Holt, Rinehart and Winston, 1970). Reprinted by permission.

16. Gary Simpkins, Grace Holt, and Charlesetta Simpkins, *Bridge: A Cross-Cultural Reading Program* (Boston: Houghton Mifflin, 1977). Reprinted by permission.

17. The version of *Shine* presented here is taken from the author's memory as he recalls hearing it as an adolescent in the Fillmore district of San Francisco in the 1950s. Other versions of *Shine* appear in Abrahams (1970), Simpkins (1977), Levine (1977), and Dance (1978).

18. R. Ames, "Protest and Irony in Negro Folksong," *Social Science,* 14 (1950), pp. 193–213. Reprinted by permission.

19. "The Story of my Life," Mary Livermore (Hartford, Conn. 1987), pp. 306–307.
20. Alan Wesson, "The Black Man's Burden: The White Clinician," *The Black Scholar*, 1975 (6), pp. 13–18. Reprinted by permission.
21. Ralph Ellison, *Invisible Man* (New York: Random House, 1952), pp. 107–111. Reprinted by permission.

CHAPTER FIVE

1. Written with assistance from Dr. William Parham, UCLA, who coauthored an earlier derivative of this chapter, Parham, W. D. and Parham, T. A., *The Community and Academic Achievement*. In G. L. Berry and J. K. Asaman (ed.), *Psychological Issues and Academic Achievement*. (Newbury Park: Sage Publications, 1989).
2. Taken from the song "I Need Love" by L. L. Cool-J., 1987, Def Jam Records.
3. Taken from the song "Au Cassanova" by Lavert, 1987, Atlantic Records.
4. Taken from the song "Shake You Down" by Gregory Abbott, 1986, Columbia Records.
5. Taken from the song "Bad" by Michael Jackson, 1987, Epic Records.

CHAPTER SEVEN

1. The theme for this quote was adapted from the Rubaiyat of Omar Khayyam. Khayyam was a Persian poet who is best known for his collection of quatrains in which the first, second, and fourth lines rhyme.
2. From the song "Ain't Noth'in Going On But the Rent" by Gwen Guthrie, 1986, Polydor Records.
3. From the song "Thanks For My Child" by Cheryl Pepsi-Riley, 1988, Columbia Records.

REFERENCES

ABRAHAMS, R. (1970). *Deep Down in the Jungle*. Chicago: Adline Publishing Co.

ADAMS, W. A. (1950). "The Negro Patient in Psychiatric Treatment," *American Journal of Orthopsychiatry*, 201, 305–308.

ADEBIMPE, V. (1981). "Overview: White Norms in Psychiatric Diagnosis of Black Patients," *American Journal of Psychiatry*, 138(3), 275–285.

AKBAR, N. (1981). *Mental Disorders Among African Americans*. Black Books Bulletin, 7(2), 18–25.

AKBAR, N. (1989). "Nigrescence and Identity: Some Limitations." *The Counseling Psychologist*. Vol 17,(2), 258–263.

American College Dictionary (1987). New York: Random House.

AMES, R. (1950). "Protest and Irony in Negro Folksong," *Social Science*, 14, 193–213.

ARIES, P. (1980). *The Hour of Our Death*. New York: Knopf.

ARNEZ, N. L. (1972). "Enhancing Black Self-Concept Through Literature." In J. Banks and J. Grambs (eds.), *Black Self-Concept*. New York: McGraw Hill.

AZIBO, D. (1989). "Advances in Black/African Personality Theory." Unpublished manuscript.

AZIBO, D. (1983). "Some Psychological Concomitants and Consequences of the Black Personality: Mental Health

Implications," *Journal of Non-White Concerns* (January), 59–66.

BALDWIN, J. A. (1985). "African Self-Consciousness Scale: An Afrocentric Questionnaire," *Western Journal of Black Studies*, (9)2, 61–68.

BALDWIN, J. (1963). *The Fire Next Time.* New York: Dell Publishing Co.

BALDWIN, J. (1965). *Going to Meet the Man.* New York: Dial Press.

BALDWIN, J. (1955). *Notes of a Native Son.* New York: Beacon Press, 1955.

BANKS, W. AND GRAMBS, J. (1972). *Black Self Concept.* New York: McGraw-Hill.

BARNES, E. J. (1972). "The Black Community as the Source of Positive Self-Concept for Black Children: A Theoretical Perspective." In R. L. Jones (ed.), *Black Psychology.* New York: Harper & Row.

BASCH, M. (1980). *Doing Psychotherapy.* New York: Basic Books.

BEEZ, W. V. (1969). "Influence of Biased Psychological Reports on Teacher Behavior and Pupil Performance." Proceedings of the 76th Annual Conventions of the American Psychological Association, No. 3, 605–606.

BERRY, G. (1982). "Television, Self-Esteem and the Afro-American Child: Some Implications for Mental Health Professionals." In B. A. Bass, G. E. Wyath, and G. J. Powell (eds.), *The Afro-American Family: Assessment, Treatment and Research Issues.* New York: Grune & Stratton.

BILLINGSLEY, A. (1968). *Black Families in White America.* Englewood Cliffs, NJ: Prentice-Hall.

BLASSINGAME, J. (1972). *The Slave Community.* New York: Oxford University Press.

BLOCK, C. (1980). "Black Americans and the Cross-Cultural Counseling Experience." In A. J. Marsella and P. B. Pederson (eds.), *Cross-Cultural Counseling and Psychotherapy.* New York: Pergamon.

BOURNE, P. (1973). "Alcoholism in the Urban Population." In P. Bourne and R. Fox (eds.), *Alcoholism: Progress in Research and Treatment*. New York: Academic Press.

BRAYBOY, T. (1971). "The Black Patient in Group Therapy." *International Journal of Group Psychotherapy*, 2(3), 288–293.

BRIGHAM, J. C. (1974). "Views of Black and White Children Concerning the Distribution of Personality Characteristics," *Journal of Personality*, 42, 144–158.

BROWN, D. (1972). *Bury My Heart at Wounded Knee*. New York: Holt, Rinehart & Winston.

BROWN, H. R. (1969). *Die Nigger Die*. New York. Dial Press.

BROWNE, C. (1973). *The Children of Ham*. Briarcliffe Manor, NY: Stein & Day, 1973.

CAMBRIDGE, G. *Here's Godfrey Cambridge, Ready or Not* (album). EPIC, Footlight Series.

CAMPBELL, D. T. (176). "Stereotypes and the Perception of Group Differences," *American Psychologists*, 22, 817–829.

CAPLAN, N. (1970). "The New Negro Man: A Review of Recent Empirical Studies," *Journal of Social Issues*, 26, 57–73.

CARMICHAEL, S. (1971). *Stokely Speaks, Black Power to Pan-Africanism*. New York: Vintage Books.

CARTER, R. and HELMS, J. E. (1987). "The Relationship of Black Value-Orientations to Racial Attitudes," *Measurement and Evaluation in Counseling and Development*, 17, 185–195.

CLAIBORN, W. L. (1969). "Expectancy Effects in the Classroom: A Failure to Replicate," *Journal of Educational Psychology*, 60, 377–383.

CLARK, C. (1975). "The Shockley-Jensen Thesis: A Contextual Appraisal," *The Black Scholar*, 6, 2–5.

CLARK, K. and CLARK, M. (1947). "Racial Identification and Preferences in Negro Children," *Readings in Social Psychology*. New York: Holt.

CLARK, M. and GOSNELL, M. "The Graying of America," *Newsweek*, February 28, 1977

CLARK, R. (1983). *Family Life and School Achievement*. Chicago: University of Chicago Press.

CLEAVER, E. (1968). *Soul on Ice*. New York: Dell Publishing Co.

COTTLE, T. A. (1975). "A Case of Suspension," *National Elementary Principal*, 5, 69–74.

COUNTER, S. A. and EVANS, D. L. (1981). *I Sought My Brother: An Afro-American Reunion*. Cambridge: MIT Press.

CROSS, W. E. (1971). "The Negro to Black Conversion Experience: Towards the Psychology of Black Liberation," *Black World*, 20, 13–27.

CROSS, W. E. (1978). "The Thomas and Cross Models of Psychological Nigrescence: A Review," *Journal of Black Psychology*, 5, 13–31.

CROSS, W. E., PARHAM, T. A., and HELMS, J. E. (eds.) "Nigrescence Revisited: Theory and Research." In R. L. Jones (ed.). In *Advances in Black Psychology*. (In press.)

DANCE, D. (1978). *Shuckin' and Jivin': Folklore from Contemporary Black Americans*. Bloomington: Indiana University Press.

DANSBY, P. (1972). "Black Pride in the Seventies: Fact or Fantasy." In R. L. Jones (ed.), *Black Psychology*. New York: Harper & Row.

DAVIS, R. (1981). "A Demographic Analysis of Suicide." In L. E. Gary (ed.), *Black Men*. Beverly Hills: Sage Publishing Company.

DAVIS, O. (1968). "The Wonderful World of Law and Order." In H. Hill (ed.), *Anger and Beyond: The Negro Writer in the United States*. New York: Harper & Row.

DuBOIS, W. E. B. (1903). *The Souls of Black Folks*. Chicago: McClurg.

DYKE, B. (1983). "Pre-Therapy Education Techniques for Black Families: Expectancies and Cognitions." Unpublished doctoral dissertation, University of Pennsylvania.

ELLISON, R. (1952). *Invisible Man*. New York: Random House.

FIESTER, A. R. and RUDESTAM, K. E. (1975). "A Multivariate Analysis of the Early Drop-Out Process," *Journal of Consulting and Clinical Psychology*, 43(4), 528–535.

FISHER, J. (1969). "Negroes and Whites and Rates of Mental Illness: Reconsideration of a Myth," *Psychiatry*, 32, 428–446.

FLEMING, E. S. and ANTTONEN, R. G. (1971). "Teacher Expectancy or My Fair Lady," *Aera Journal*, 8, 241.

FRAZIER, E. F. (1962). *Black Bourgeoisie*. New York: Crowell, Collier and MacMillan.

FRAZIER, E. F. (1939). *The Negro Family in the United States*. Chicago: University of Chicago Press.

FREDERICKSON, G. (1976). "The Gutman Report," *The New York Times Review*, September 30, 18–22, 27.

GIBBS, J. T. (1988). *Young, Black, and Male in America*. Dover, MA: Audburn House Publishing Company.

GOODLAD, J. (1983). *A Place Called Schools: Prospects for the Future*. New York: McGraw Hill.

GOODMAN, M. E. (1952). *Racial Awareness in Young Children*. Cambridge: Addison Wesley.

GREENBERG, B. and DERVIN, B. (1970). "Mass Communication Among the Urban Poor," *Public Opinion Quarterly*, 34, 224–235.

GRIER, W. H., COBBS, P. M. (1968). *Black Rage*. New York: Basic Books.

GURIN, P. and EPPS, E. (1975). *Black Consciousness, Identity, and Achievement: A Study of Students in Historically Black Colleges*. New York: John Wiley & Sons.

GUTMAN, H. (1976). *The Black Family in Slavery and Freedom: 1750–1925*. New York: Vintage Books.

HALBERSTAM, D. (1971). *The Best and the Brightest*. New York: Random House.

HARAYDA, J. (1987). "How to Be Happy Single," *Essence*, 18(6) (October), 61–62.

HARE, N. (1965). *Black Anglo-Saxons*. New York: Mangi and Mansell.

HARPER, F. D. (1979). *Alcoholism Treatment and Black Americans*. Rockville, MD: Department of Health, Education and Welfare, National Institute on Alcohol Abuse and Alcoholism.

HARPER, F. D. (1981). "Alcohol Use and Abuse." In L. E. Gary (ed.), *Black Men*. Beverly Hills, CA: Sage Publishing Company.

HEITLER, J. (1976). "Preparatory Techniques in Initiating Expressive Group Therapy with Lower-Class, Unsophisticated Patients," *Psychological Bulletin*, 83(2), 339–352.

HELMS, J. E. (1984). "Toward a Theoretical Explanation of the Effects of Race on Counseling: A Black and White Model," *Counseling Psychologists*, 12(4), 153–165.

HIGHLEN, P. S. and HILL, C. E. (1984). "Factors Affecting Client Change in Individual Counseling: Current Status of Theoretical Speculations." In S. D. Brown and R. W. Lent (eds.), *The Handbook of Counseling Psychology*. New York: John Wiley & Sons.

HILL, R. (1971). *Strengths of the Black Family*. New York: National Urban League.

HILLIARD, T. (1972). "Personality Characteristics of Black Student Activists and Non-Activists." In R. L. Jones (ed.), *Black Psychology*. New York: Harper & Row.

HINES, P. M. and BOYD-FRANKLIN, N. (1982). "Black Families." In M. McGoldrick, V. Pearce, and J. Giordane (eds.), *Ethnicity in Family Therapy*. New York: Guilford Press.

HOLT, G. (1975). "Metaphor, Black Discourse Style and Cultural Reality." In R. L. Williams (ed.), *Ebonics, the True Language of Black Folks*. St. Louis: Institute of Black Studies.

HUGHES, L. (1954). "Mother to Son." In *Selected Poems by Langston Hughes*. New York: Knopf.

HUGHES, L. (1950). *Simple Speaks His Mind.* New York: Simon & Schuster.

HUGHES, L. (1953). *Simple Takes a Wife.* New York: Simon & Schuster.

HUGHES, L. (1957). *Simple Takes a Claim.* New York: Holt, Rinehart & Winston.

JACKSON, B. (1976). "Black Identity Development." In L. Gloubshick and B. Persky (eds.), *Urban Social and Educational Issues.* Dubuque: Kendall-Hall, 158–164.

JACKSON, M. (1968). "How I Got Over." In *Mahalia Jackson Sings the Best-Loved Hymns of Dr. Martin Luther King, Jr.* (album). New York: Columbia Records.

JEFFERS, L. (1971). "Afro-American Literature, The Conscience of Man," *The Black Scholar* (January 1971), 47–53.

JENSEN, A. (1969). "How Much Can We Boost I.Q. and Scholastic Achievement?" *Harvard Educational Review*, 39, 1–123.

JEWELL, K. S. (1988). *Survival of the Black Family: The Institutional Impact of U.S. Social Policy.* New York: Praeger.

JOHNSON, J. (1983). "Why Black Men Have the Highest Cancer Rate," *Ebony* (March), 69–72.

JONES, L. (1963). *Blues People: Negro Music in White America.* New York: Morrow.

KARDINER, A. and OVESSEY, L. (1951). *The Mark of Oppression.* New York: Norton.

KARENGA, M. (1976). *Kwanzaa, Origin, Concepts, Practice.* Los Angeles: Kawaida Publications.

KERNER, O. (Chairman) (1968). *Report of the National Commission on Civil Disorders: U.S. Riot Commission Report.* New York: Bantam Books.

KING, L. (1982). "Suicide from a Black Reality Perspective." In B. Bass, G. E. Wyatt, and G. Powell (eds.), *The Afro-American Family: Assessment, Treatment and Research.* New York: Grune and Stratton.

KING, M. L., Jr. (1971). "I Have a Dream" (speech delivered at the March on Washington, August 1963). In A. Meier, E. Rudwick, and F. L. Brokerick (eds.), *Black Protest Thought in the Twentieth Century*, 2nd Ed. New York: Bobbs-Merrill.

KLUCKJOHN, F. R. and STRODTBECK, F. L. (1961). *Variations in Value Orientations*. Evanston, IL: Row, Peterson.

KNIGHT, G. (1973). "I've Got to Use My Imagination." In *Imagination* (album). New York: Buddha Records.

KINCAID, M. (1968). "Identity and Therapy in the Black Community," *Personnel and Guidance Journal*, 47, 884–890.

KUNJUFU, J. (1986). *Motivating and Preparing Black Youth to Work*. Chicago: African American Images.

LADNER, J. (1971). *Tomorrow's Tomorrow: The Black Woman*. Garden City: Doubleday.

LESTER, J. (1971). "The Angry Children of Malcolm X." In T. Fraizer (ed.), *Afro-American History Primary Sources*. New York: Harcourt Brace Jovanovich.

LEVINE, L. (1971). *Black Culture and Black Consciousness: Afro-American Folk Thought from Slavery to Freedom*. New York: Oxford University Press.

LEWIS, D. (1971). *King, A Critical Biography*. Baltimore: Penguin.

LIVERMORE, M. (1897). *The Story of My Life*. Hartford, Ct.

LOMAX, L. (1961). "The American Negro's New Comedy Act," *Harper* (June), 41–46.

MALCOLM X. (1965). *The Autobiography of Malcolm X*. New York: Grove Press.

MARTINEZ, J. L. (ed.) (1977) *Chicano Psychology*. New York: Academic Press.

MBITI, J. S. (1970). *African Religions and Philosophies*. Garden City, New York: Anchor Books.

MCADOO, H. P. (1979). "Black Kinship," *Psychology Today*, May, 67–69, 79, 110.

MCADOO, H. P. (ed.) (1981). *Black Families*. Beverly Hills: Sage Publications.

MCADOO, H. P. (1978). "Factors Related to Stability in Upwardly Mobile Black Families," *Journal of Marriage and Family*, 40, 761–778.

MCADOO, H. P. (1981). "Upward Mobility and Parenting in Middle-Income Black Families," *Journal of Black Psychology*, 8(1), 1–22.

MCCORD, W., HOWARD, J., FRIEDBERG, B., and HARWOOD, E. (1969). *Lifestyles in the Black Ghetto*. New York: W. W. Norton.

MITCHELL, H. (1989). "The Black Family: Five Generational Model for Continuity and Enhancement." Unpublished manuscript.

MOORE, E. K. (1981). "Policies Affecting the States of Black Children and Families." In H. P. McAdoo (ed.), *Black Families*. Beverly Hills: Sage Publications.

MOORE-CAMPBELL, B. (1987). "Breaking the Age Taboo," *Essence*, 17(10) (February), 51–52, 108.

MORELAND, J. K. (1958). "Racial Recognition by Nursery School Children," *Social Forces*, 37, 132–137.

MOYNIHAN, D. (1965). *The Negro Family: The Case for National Action*. Washington, D.C.: Office of Policy Planning and Research, U.S. Department of Labor.

MURRELL, S. (1978). *Community Psychology and Social Systems: A Conceptual Framework and Intervention Guide*. New York: Behavioral Publications.

MYERS, H. F. (1982). "Research on the Afro-American Family: a Critical Review." In B. Bass, G. E. Wyatt, and G. Powell, *The Afro-American Family: Assessment, Treatment and Research*. New York: Grune and Stratton.

MYERS, L. J. (1985). "Transpersonal Psychology: The Role of the Afrocentric Paradigm," *Journal of Black Psychology*, 12(1), 31–42.

Myes, H. J. and Yochelson, L. (1949). "Color Denial in the Negro," *Psychiatry*, 11, 39–42.

National Center for Health Statistics (1979). *Health*. Washington, D.C.: Government Printing Office.

National Commission on Excellence in Education (1983). *A Nation at Risk: The Imperative for Educational Reform*. Washington, D.C.: Government Printing Office.

Neal, L. (1972). "The Ethos of the Blues," *The Black Scholar* (Summer), 42–48.

Nobles, W. (1974). "Africanity: Its Role in Black Families," *The Black Scholar*, June, 10–17.

Nobles, W. (1972). *African Philosophy: Foundation for Black Psychology*. N. R. L. Jones (ed.), *Black Psychology*. New York: Harper & Row.

Nobles, W. (1986). *African Psychology: Towards Its Reclamation, and Revitalization*. Oakland: Black Family Institute.

Nobles, W. (1976). "Black People in White Insanity: An Issue for Community Mental Health," *Journal of Afro-American Issues*, 4(1) (Winter), 21–27.

Nobles, W. (1976). "Extended-Self: Rethinking the So-called Negro Self-Concept," *Journal of Black Psychology*, 11(2).

Nobles, W. (1977). "The Rhythmic Impulse: The Issue of Africanity in Black Family Dynamics." Paper presented to the second annual symposium on Black Psychology, Ann Arbor, Michigan.

Nobles, W. (1978). "Toward an Empirical and Theoretical Framework for Defining Black Families," *Journal of Marriage and Family*. November, 679–688.

Norton, D. G. (no date). "Black Family Life Patterns, the Development of Self and Cognitive Development of Black Children." In Powell, Yavrstate, and Morales (eds.), *The Psychosocial Development of Minority Group Children*.

PALARDY, J. M. (1969). "What Teachers Believe—What Children Achieve," *Elementary School Journal*, 69, 370–374.

PARHAM, T. A. and MCDAVIS, R. (1987). "Black Males and Endangered Species: Who's Really Pulling the Trigger?" *Journal of Counseling and Development*, 66, 24–27.

PARHAM, T. A. (1989). "Cycles of Psychological Nigrescence," *The Counseling Psychologist.* 17(2), 187–226.

PARHAM, T. A. and HELMS, J. E. (1981). "Influences of Black Student's Racial Identity Attitudes on Preferences for Counselor Race," *Journal of Counseling Psychology*, 28(3), 250–256.

PARHAM, T. A. and HELMS, J. E. (1985). "Relation of Racial Identity to Self-Actualization and Affective States of Black Students," *Journal of Counseling Psychiatry*, 28(3), 250–256.

PATTON, J. M. (1981). "The Black Male's Struggle for an Education." In L. E. Gary (ed.), *Black Men.* Beverly Hills, CA: Sage Publications.

PEARL, A. and RIESSMAN, F. (1965). *New Careers for the Poor.* New York: Free Press.

PEDERSEN, P. B. (1982). "Alternative Futures for Cross Cultural Counseling and Psychotherapy." In A. J. Marsella and B. P. Pedersen (eds.), *Cross Cultural Counseling and Pschotherapy.* New York: Pergamon.

PETTIGREW, W. (1964). "Negro American Personality: Why Isn't More Known?" *Journal of Social Issues*, 20, 4–23.

PIDGEON, D. A. (1970). *Expectations and Pupil Performance.* Washington, D.C. National Federation for Educational Research.

POUSSAINT, A. F. (1972). *Why Blacks Kill Blacks.* New York: Emerson Hall.

POWELL, G. J. (1973). "Self-Concept in White and Black Children." In C. B. Willie, B. M. Kramer, and B. S. Brown (eds.), *Racism and Mental Health.* Pittsburgh: University of Pittsburgh.

POWELL, G. J. and FULLER, M. (1970). "Self-Concept and School Desegration," *American Journal of Orthopsychiatry*, 40, 303.

PRYOR, R. (1975). "Mudbone." In *Richard Pryor, Is It Something I Said?* (album) New York: Reprise Records.

PRYOR, R. (1977). *Richard Pryor's Greatest Hits* (album). New York: Warner Brothers Records.

PUGH, R. (1972). *Psychology of the Black Experience.* Belmont, CA: Wadsworth.

RAINWATER, L. (1970). *Behind Ghetto Walls: Black Family Life in a Federal Slum.* Chicago: Aldine.

RAY, E. C. (1989). "Lifestyle: Commuter Marriage: Does It Work?" *Essence*, 19(10) (February), 103, 107–108.

REDMOND, E. (1971). "The Black American Epic: Its Roots, Its Writers," *The Black Scholar* (January), 15–22.

RICHARDSON, E. (1981). "Cultural and Historical Perspectives in Counseling American Indians." In D. W. Sue, *Counseling the Culturally Different.* New York: John Wiley & Sons.

ROGERS, C. (1961). *On Becoming a Person.* Boston: Houghton Mifflin.

ROGERS, D. (1978). *Adolescence: A Psychological Perspective*, 2nd Ed. Monterey, CA: Brook Cole.

ROSENBERG, M. (1979). *Conceiving of Self.* New York: Basic Books.

ROSENTHAL, R. and JACOBSON, L. (1968). *Pygmalion in the Classroom.* New York: Holt, Rinehart & Winston.

ROTHBART, M., DALFEN, S., and BARRETT, R. (1971). "Effects of Teacher Expectancy on Student-Teacher Interaction," *Journal of Educational Psychology*, 62, 1, 49–54.

RUBOVITZ, P. C. and MAEHR, M. L. (1973). "Pygmalion Black and White," *Journal of Personality and Social Psychology*, 25, 2, 210–218.

SAMAJ, L. (1981). "The Black Self: Identity and Models for a Psychology of Black Liberation," *Western Journal of Black Studies*, 5(3), 158–171.

SCHLESINGER, A. Jr. (1978). *Robert Kennedy and His Times*. Boston: Houghton Mifflin.

SHIPP, P. (1983). "Counseling Blacks: A Group Approach," *Personnel and Guidance Journal*, 62(2), 108–111.

SIMPKINS, G., HOLT, G., and SIMPKINS, C. (1977). *Bridge, A Cross-Cultural Reading Program*. Boston: Houghton Mifflin.

SMITH, E. (1977). "Counseling Black Individuals: Some Strategies," *Personnel and Guidance Journal*, 55, 390–396.

SMITH, E. (1974). "Evolution and Continuing Presence of the Oral Tradition of Black America." Doctoral dissertation submitted to the University of California, Irvine.

SMITHERMAN, G. *Talkin and Testifyin: The Language of Black America*. Boston: Houghton Mifflin.

SPILLERS, H. (1971). "Martin Luther King and the Style of the Black Sermon," *The Black Scholar* (September), 14–27.

STACKS, G. (1974). *All Our Kin: Strategies or Survival in the Black Community*. New York: Harper & Row.

STAPLES, R. (1982). *Black Masculinity*. San Francisco: Black Scholar Press.

SUDARKASA, N. (1981). "Interpreting the African Heritage in Afro-American Family Organization." In H. P. McAdoo (ed.), *Black Families*. Beverly Hills: Sage Publications.

SUE, S. (1978). "Ethnic Minority Research: Trends and Directions." Paper presented at National Conference on Minority Group Alcohol, Druag Abuse and Mental Health Issues, Denver.

SUE, S. and WAGNER, N. (1973) (eds.) *Asian Americans: Psychological Perspectives*. Palo Alto, CA: Science and Behavior Books.

SUE, S. (1977). "Community Mental Health Service to Minority Groups," *American Psychologist*, 32, 616–624.

SUE, D. W. (1981). *Counseling the Culturally Different*. New York: John Wiley & Sons.

Task Force on Education for Economic Growth (1983). *Action for Excellence: A Comprehensive Plan to Improve Our*

Nation's Schools. Denver: Educational Commission of the States.

THOMAS, A. and SILLEN, S. (1972). *Racism and Psychiatry.* Secaucus, NJ: The Citadel Press.

THOMAS, C. (1971). *Boys No More.* Beverly Hills: Glenco Press.

THOMAS, G. (1977). *Access to Higher Education: How Important Are Race, Sex, Social Class, and Academic Credentials for College?* Baltimore: Johns Hopkins Press.

THOMAS, W. (1967). *The Thomas Self-Concept Values Test: For Children Ages 3–9.* Grand Rapids, MI: Educational Service.

WARREN, R. P. (1965). *Who Speaks for the Negro?* New York: Random House.

WASHINGTON, E. D. (1932). *Selected Speeches of Booker T. Washington.* New York: Kraus Reprints Co.

WEINBERG, M. (1977). *Minority Students: A Research Appraisal.* Washington, D.C.: USDHEW, National Institute of Education.

WESSON, A. (1975). "The Black Man's Burden: The White Clinician," *The Black Scholar,* 6, 13–18.

WHITE, J. L. (1972). "Toward a Black Psychology." In R. L. Jones (ed.), *Black Psychology.* New York: Harper & Row.

WHITE, J. L. (1984). *The Psychology of Blacks: An Afro-American Perspective.* Englewood Cliffs, NJ: Prentice-Hall.

WITHERS, B. (1971). "Grandma's Hands." In *Bill Withers Live at Carnegie Hall* (album). Hollywood: Sussex Records.

WILLIAMS, R. (1974). *Cognitive and Social Learning of the Black Child: The Survival of Black Children and Youth.* Washington, D.C.: Science Publications.

WILLIAMS, R. (1975). *Textbook of Black-Related Diseases.* New York: McGraw Hill.

WILLIAMS, R. L. (1981). *Collective Black Mind: An Afrocentric Theory of Black Personality.* St. Louis: Williams & Associates, Inc.

WRIGHT, R. (1945). *Black Boy.* New York: Harper & Row.

WRIGHT, R. (1977). *American Hunger*. New York: Harper & Row.

WYLIE, R. (1978). *The Self-Concept*, rev. ed. (*Vol. 2: Theory and Research on Selected Topics*). Lincoln: University of Nebraska Press.

WYNE, M. D., WHITE, K. D., COOP, R. H. (1974). *The Black Self*. Englewood Cliffs, NJ: Prentice-Hall.

YALOM, I. (1975). *The Theory and Practice of Group Psychotherapy*. New York: Basic Books.

ZAX, M. and SPECTER, G. (1974). *Introduction to Community Psychology*. New York: John Wiley & Sons.

INDEX